A MOST PRECIOUS
Message

My
personal
discovery
of liberating joy
in the
gospel of Jesus

JENNIFER
JILL
SCHWIRZER

Pacific Press® Publishing Association
Nampa, Idaho
Oshawa, Ontario, Canada

Edited by Jerry D. Thomas
Designed by Tim Larson
Cover photo by Crystal Montgomery ©

Copyright © 2001 by
Pacific Press® Publishing Association
Printed in United States of America
All Rights Reserved

Unless otherwise indicated, Scripture quotations are taken from the New American Standard Version.

ISBN: 0-8163-1841-7

01 02 03 04 05 • 5 4 3 2 1

Contents

CHAPTER ONE

Goody Two-Shoes Gets the Gospel

I converted to Christianity at nineteen years of age. A born-again believer, I set out to find a church that could answer my many burning questions about life, death, love, God, and the way He wanted me to live. Nine months later I was a Seventh-day Adventist.

I converted to Adventism through the ministry of what most of us would call an "ultra conservative" group. For ten years afterwards, I preached vegan vegetarianism (still do), country living (still love it), modesty, simplicity and primitive piety (still believe in them), and Christ.

The problem was, sometimes it was in that order. In other words, the lifestyle cart was before the gospel horse.

Don't get me wrong. I was a deeply converted Christian. It's just that in many ways, I was like the Galatian goody-goodies who had "begun in the spirit," but thought I was "being perfected by the flesh." Fortunately, the legalistic period of my life had a function. Goody two-shoes was "kept in custody under the law, being shut up to the faith which was later to be revealed" (Galatians 3:23). For a time the standards were my safety zone, the rules and regulations were my righteousness, but I was "shut up," or reserved, for something that would be revealed . . . "later."

God allowed me to try to earn salvation in order to find out that I never could.

God allowed me to exhaust the possibilities of human effort for ten years before He brought me face to face with the truth of righteousness by faith.

Sometimes I'm afraid to use that well-worn term. I'm a right-brainer, a poet, a non-conformist at heart. I like saying things in an unorthodox way. Besides that, after several decades of tossing the term around, the infatuation has subsided for most of us. As far as the jargon goes, the thrill is gone.

But here I am using the term. Why? Because while we may have run the *term* "righteousness by faith" into the ground, we haven't even begun to exhaust the *teaching.* Let me use myself as a case in point. I was a Seventh-day Adventist for ten years before I could tell you the following: "Works are a fruit of salvation and not a means of it."

This simple, basic tenet of the gospel was not clear in my mind. I remember toward the end of my first ten years as a Seventh-day Adventist Christian writing a song for children called "Very Special Friend," with the following lyrics:

> *Do you know the truest Friend of all?*
> *He is a very special Friend*
> *He will love you even if you fall*
> *That is why He is the truest Friend of all*

I gasped as I read the words I had written. I was filled with doubt, imploring my own conscience, "Is that true? Does God love us *even if we fall?* If I say that, won't it give people license to sin?" But as I reasoned objectively through my poem, I knew it had to be true. God is love, and so He loves at all times, sin or not. Try as I might, I could not fault my poem, and so I lifted my pen from the page. I would leave it as it was. But isn't it amazing? Something so simple as God's unfailing love for sinners had eluded me until I stumbled upon it as I tried to force a rhyme. If the teaching of justification by faith were all-pervasive, it would have reached me before the ten-year mark of my Adventist experience.

The same is true of the scores of people I talk to and counsel with in the course of ministry. So many do not really know the simple rest that comes from security in Christ. They are guilt-wracked, stress-ridden, and fearful of condemnation from God and other church members. The *term* "righteousness by faith" or "justification by faith" does nothing to alleviate their distress, but clear *teaching* of the doctrine would be like an antidote to a snakebite victim. And as long as the serpent lives, the message will never lose its power, its relevance, or its takers.

OK, I'll admit that part of the problem was my own complacency. While I was perfect, I didn't see my need for the message of Christ's righteousness. And I was perfect for quite a while, making significant sacrifices to achieve this status. I'll tell you a little about those sacrifices.

Female modesty was probably what I considered my most meritorious offering. I sewed strips of fabric around the bottom of my already long dresses once when I came into contact with a group of women who thought dresses should be two inches longer than mine were. The strips didn't match very well, but then I didn't want to be vain. The same women influenced me to wear my long hair pinned up in a barrette, which I wore for so long that I developed a bald spot. I had devotions every morning for exactly one hour, feeling that if I didn't, some catastrophe would strike that day.

Again, don't get me wrong. I still think standards are important. I am forever indebted to the people who first introduced me to the principles of Christian living as put forth in the Bible and the Spirit of Prophecy. But I think the fear motivation led me to interpret those principles with an exactitude that was at times self-defeating. "The letter kills, but the Spirit gives life" (2 Corinthians 3:6).

Some of my friends viewed my "conversion" to justification by faith with concern because it made me secure enough to relax my rigidity. For them, anything that took a person away from the strictest scruples was to be shunned. They wanted proof in the pudding, and the pudding had to be sugar, dairy, and chemical free. I tried to convince them that the real proof was the test of Galatians 5:14, "for the whole Law is fulfilled in one word, . . . [that] "You shall love your neighbor as yourself.' " Love is the ultimate expression of the law of love, I pointed out.

I remember recognizing a brazen *lack* of love in the midst of the conservative community I was a part of. Adultery. Theft. Murder in the form of hate. All carried out under a guise of holiness. " 'Woe to you, scribes and Pharisees, hypocrites! For you are like whitewashed tombs which on the outside appear beautiful, but inside they are full of dead men's bones and all uncleanness' " (Matthew 23:27).

You may shake your head in response to sensational accounts of "fanatics" like me, but remember that the principle of righteousness by works has more than one manifestation. There is a conservative flavor, a middle of the road flavor, and even a liberal flavor. Being more moderate in the lifestyle areas will not succeed in delivering you from legalism, for legalism is in your very bones. If you don't resort to nineteenth-century dresses, starvation diets, and superstitious Bible study, you will find a milder way to express your works program—perhaps by taking pride in your prayer meeting and church attendance or paying a faithful tithe or studying your lesson every day. Or maybe you will become legalistic about not being legalistic. I know plenty of legalists whose favorite rule is not to have any rules.

Whatever masquerade it shows up in, legalism is the same bandit underneath, which is why we need a constant and ever-fresh revelation of the gospel. The good news of God's salvation is designed to "lay the ax to the root of the tree" of self-salvation, that soil of the heart may be freed forever from its domination.

Why do so many of us still struggle with thinking that standards will save us? Is it the standards' fault? Seventh-day Adventists have more "moral admonition" than most people, meaning we have more *dos* and *don'ts*. The Bible is a good start, but Ellen White's writings add to the list with 25 million words that deal with everything from preaching to pickles. This counsel, meant to be a blessing, has become a burden to many because it is not understood in the light of God's love. The legalities loom large as the good news is obscured. A few strong-willed ones keep up the pace, while the majority languish in self-defeat. A good-sized contingency becomes shell-shocked and hardened to any and all admonition. Restraint imposed from without, breeds anger into the heart. Anger boils over into rebellion. We so often become living proof that "the law worketh wrath" (Romans 4:15, KJV).

Considering the potentially harmful side effects of rules, we are tempted to wonder why God gave us so many—but the fact is that God never meant for those admonitions and counsels to stand alone. He wished for us to see all the restraints as *con*straints of love, all the commandments as promises. It can be hazardous to our spiritual health to see the law as detached from love. In fact, it can be fatal![1] This is why the teaching of Christ's righteousness should be at front and center of all of our communications.

Legalism can't be simply extracted—it must be displaced. No one can bear to live without some form of righteousness! This is why Adam and Eve's first compulsion after sin was to manufacture their own garments of self-defense. Experiencing a complete understanding of their fallen condition would have produced a self-annihilating insanity, but denial temporarily saved them from this awareness. We have inherited the same denial, which we need as a defense mechanism against madness until such a time as we receive righteousness from its only true Source. So because we can't bear to be without any righteousness at all, the only way to pry our fingers off our self-righteousness is to dangle the righteousness of Christ before our tired eyes. Then the grip loosens as naturally as a child's on a forgotten toy.

After a season of youthful self-confidence, I found myself disillusioned with others and myself. Good people weren't so good after all, and come to think of it, neither was I. The works program, as unconscious as it was, had consumed me, chewed me up, and then spit me out. Thank God, He replaced my broken toys with a Gift beyond my wildest dreams. That Gift was in the form of a message that I now call "most precious."

Brethren, shall we not all of us leave our loads there? And when we leave this meeting, may it be with the truth burning in our souls like fire shut up in our bones. You will meet with those who will say, 'You are too much excited over this matter. You are too much in earnest. You should not be reaching for the righteousness of Christ, and making so much of that. You should preach the law.' As a people, we have preached the law until we are as dry as the hills of Gilboa that had neither dew nor rain. We must preach Christ in the law, and there will be sap and nourishment in the preaching that will be as food to the famishing flock of God. We must not trust in our own merits at all, but in the merits of Jesus of Nazareth. Our eyes must be anointed with eye-salve. We must draw nigh to God, and he will draw nigh to us, if we come in his own appointed way. O that you may go forth as the disciples did after the day of Pentecost, and then your testimony will have a living ring, and souls will be converted to God.[2]

---

1. *"I was once alive apart from the Law; but when the commandment came, sin revived and I died. And this commandment, which was to result in life, proved to result in death for me; for sin, taking opportunity through the commandment, deceived me, and through it killed me"* (see Romans 7:9-11). Forgive the liberty I take with that verse. Consider it a "spiritualization" of the text. Anecdotal evidence, however, substantiates my interpretation; the law, designed as a blessing, becomes a curse when divorced from its mate, the gospel.

2. *Advent Review and Sabbath Herald*, March 11, 1890.

CHAPTER TWO

Is the 1888 Message Christ-centered?

The above-mentioned date provokes an alarm reaction for some of you. Actually, it may spur a gamut of responses from indifference to joy to migraines. Usually, this is not due to the subject itself, but rather to the controversy that surrounds it. It seems that when it is mentioned, many Adventists feel compelled to express an opinion about it. I don't have anything against opinions, but I would like to approach the subject a little differently. Rather than merely sharing what I *think* about the message, I want to share what I have *experienced* in relation to it. Of course, I will divulge my thoughts in the process, but my main purpose is to share what I know in the experiential sense. It is my hope that when you are finished, you will discard me and go study the message for yourself.

As I mentioned, a spiritual crisis of sorts led me to investigate the whole 1888 thing. I recall times when the Spirit would move me to a realization that something was missing in my religion. Here is one such time:

I was riding home in a van full of people one evening from a long day of work at a self-supporting restaurant ministry. It was Friday. Normally on Friday nights, we had a worship service in the big living room of a mansion that housed about twenty-five of the staff. This was the high point of the week. We would sing hymns until we were hoarse, then one-by-one share witnessing stories from the past week. Our sessions were punctuated with laughter and sometimes tears, filled with a kind of irrepressible excitement that I miss to this day.

When we finished the hour-plus session of sharing, someone, usually the director, would share a spiritual thought or two and then give a report of the worldwide restaurant mission field. We would hear of similar ministries being developed in faraway France, England, and even Austria, as well as all over the U.S. Awestruck, we felt to our depths that restaurant work was on the cutting edge. We believed that God was using us mightily. In fact, we thought we were at the forefront of the finishing of the Great Commission. We were young and cocky.

On this particular van ride, I remember asking who was speaking for worship that night. When one of the men volunteered that he had been chosen, I found myself blurting something out almost against my will. "Could you talk about the Cross? We haven't heard about the Cross in so long! Please talk about the Cross!"

I realized that we had been like wedding guests who, caught up in the festivities, forgot who was getting married. It is truly remarkable how human beings can get so absorbed in religion that they forget God. But for me the constant rehearsal of man's works was beginning to lose its luster, and I found myself yearning to hear about God's work.

This is why I identified, a short time later, with a statement from the pen of E. J. Waggoner about his own similar moment of truth.

I was sitting a little apart from the body of the congregation in the large tent at a camp meeting in Healdsburg (California), one gloomy Sabbath afternoon. I have no idea what was the subject of the discourse. Not a word nor a text have I ever known. All that has remained with me was what I saw. Suddenly a light shown round me, and the tent was for me far more brilliantly lighted than if the noon-day sun had been shining, and I saw Christ hanging on the cross, crucified for me. In that moment I had my first positive knowledge, which came like an overwhelming flood, that God loved me, and that Christ died for me. God and I were the only beings I was conscious of in the universe. I knew then, by actual sight, that God was in Christ reconciling the world unto Himself, and I was the whole work with all its sin. I am sure that Paul's experience on the way to Damascus was no more real than mine . . .[1]

Waggoner's moment of truth came when he realized that the Cross was everything to him. Perhaps because his sentiments and mine were so resonant, I soon decided to investigate what it was that he taught, which Ellen White said was designed to "bring more prominently before the people the uplifted Saviour."[2] This need for the uplifted Christ was universal and time-transcendent, as palpable to me in the 1980s as it had been to him in the days of horse and buggy.

I recalled a small study group years before that met early in the morning and read a small book called *The Sufferings of Christ*—one of the richest study experiences I had ever had. I could hardly call myself a theologian at this time, but I instinctively knew that the subject of the atonement held the golden key that would unlock all truth to my understanding. And I knew that the Cross would tell me like nothing else could of the love of God. I was on safe ground here. If the 1888 message would bring "more prominently before" me "the uplifted Saviour," then perhaps I should understand the 1888 message. Perhaps I should give this man, Ellet J. Waggoner, and his partner, Alonzo T. Jones, a fair hearing.

But there were challenges. When I first met Jones and Waggoner, I asked them (not in person, obviously), "Why should I read your antiquated tomes and century-old sermons? How can they possibly be relevant to me today? You didn't even know what a 'drive-by shooting' was! Or AIDS! Or the Cold War! Besides, I have a Bible and piles of Spirit of Prophecy books that I *know* are inspired, why should I read something that wasn't written by a prophet? What claim do you have to my reading time?"

Alonzo and Ellet were sleeping and couldn't answer me, but the Word spoke up in their behalf. It said, "And God has appointed in the church, first apostles, second prophets, third teachers, then miracles, then gifts of healings, helps, administrations, various kinds of tongues" (1 Corinthians 12:28). Third in the lineup of spiritual gifts was teaching, right there next to the gift of prophecy. Truly God gives certain men and women the gift of teaching. One gift is not greater than another, but all work together to bring about the optimal functioning of the body of Christ. Jones and Waggoner may not have been prophets, I realized, but they were blessed with the gift of teaching.

But why should I listen to *these particular* teachers? This was my next question.

Fortunately, my study began in the early 1990s. At the 1888 Centennial celebration, held in Minneapolis in 1988, the White Estate had released a four-volume set of all the writings of Ellen White that concerned the 1888 conference. Letters, articles, and testimonies were copied and bound together, and read by probably very few. However, because of my desire to know the truth about 1888, I gladly read them cover to tedious cover. I went in with the premise that the 1888 message was significant to Adventists today, and I came out with every doubt removed. The source of my confidence? The sheer number and vigor of the affirmations that came from the prophet concerning what these young men were teaching. Among the hundreds of her endorsements were:

"It bears divine credentials, and its fruit is unto holiness."[3]

"Light and freedom and the outpouring of the Spirit of God have attended the work."[4]

"[They are] Christ's delegated messengers."[5]

God gave these men the message they bore, but there were problems with its reception. Long-entrenched views kept many hearts closed to something that would require a change in the current of their thoughts. Leaders were affronted by the thought of two young upstarts taking the reins, and all the more alarmed when the young men presented new ideas. To be fair, Jones and Waggoner had their own combative tendencies to overcome. For all of these reasons and more, there was a drum-roll tension in the air of the 1888 conference—something big, something historical, something pivotal, was about to happen.

And it did. Second to 1844, 1888 is the most discussed and debated date in Adventism. All attempts to quash or mitigate its significance have only served to agitate the issue. It's like a family secret in some ways, bringing embarrassment and shame and therefore spoken of in hushed tones. But is it best for us to cover the past even if it divulges our denominational foibles? Isn't our purpose to vindicate God and His truth? Isn't the best way to do that to reveal the fact that He continues to strive with us in *spite* of our mistakes? "For what if some did not believe? Will their unbelief make the faithfulness of God without effect? Certainly not! Indeed, let God be true but every man a liar" (Romans 3:3, 4, NKJV).

I want to be honest. Sometimes I cringe when I refer to "1888." I am afraid I will come across as a "special interest groupie" in Adventism, someone with a sub-cultural agenda who thrives on muckraking, or perhaps someone whose sense of self is fortified by having something that other church member's don't. I certainly have enough of that in my nature to tremble at the thought! In fact, human beings are innately self-exalting and will grasp at anything we might use to establish some kind of superiority, including knowledge, which 1 Corinthians 8:1 tells us, "puffs up" (NKJV). My natural tendency is to take any knowledge I have, including my convictions and my understanding of the 1888 message, and lord it over my brothers and sisters. I am so very concerned about this possibility that I have a whole chapter devoted to it later in this book.

But there is another mistake we can make in regards to knowledge. I am aware that some people wish we could stop talking about all these confusing dates, times, places, people, and theological split ends and just "focus on Jesus," and I agree with them. This is exactly the point! This message was designed to "bring more prominently" before our eyes the "uplifted Saviour"—in short, to focus our eyes upon Jesus. Christ-centeredness is not achieved through repeating His name over and over like a meaningless mantra, refusing to delve into complex historical and doctrinal issues because they may cause conflict or provoke change.

This form of "Christ-centeredness" is responsible for more ignorance of Christ than anything, because it sets the satiety point for knowledge at its lowest. Rather, Christ-centeredness is a product of a rich understanding of the gospel that is based upon unshakable, inspired facts. The issue is not how much we know, but how willing we are to learn. Jesus taught that willingness was the prerequisite for discovery of truth. (See John 7:17.)

Because of the inheritance of truth bequeathed to Seventh-day Adventists, we are in the very best position to comprehend Christ, His mission, His sacrifice, and His high priestly ministry. The 1888 message was given to build upon this foundation and further flesh out our denominational sculpture of Christ. While on the surface "1888" may appear to be an impedance to Christ-centeredness, I have found it to be the opposite. Honest seekers find it to be more attractive than detractive. So many students of 1888, including myself, fall in love with Jesus all over again.

This obscure conference, that for all appearances should have passed unmarked into the archives of Seventh-day Adventist history, still occupies the tongues and pens of thousands of SDA laypersons, scholars, educators, thinkers, and even poets. Why can't we live it down? Why can't we forget?

Perhaps the answer to these "why's" is the same as the answer to others. Why did Ellen White sit on the front pew at the 1888 conference, face aglow, so thrilled that she later wrote, "every fiber of my heart said amen"?[6] Why, in the years following, did she write a total of 1,821 pages of commentary regarding the message and its surrounding issues? Why did she say only a few years later that the message could have prepared the Church and the world for the coming of Christ?

In short, what was so great about 1888?

Please keep reading and let me try to answer that question.

The Lord in His great mercy sent a most precious message to His people through Elders Waggoner and Jones. This message was to bring more prominently before the world the uplifted Saviour, the sacrifice for the sins of the whole world. It presented justification through faith in the Surety; it invited the people to receive the righteousness of Christ, which is made manifest in obedience to all the commandments of God. Many had lost sight of Jesus. They needed to have their eyes directed to His divine person, His merits, and His changeless love for the human family. All power is given into His hands, that He may dispense rich gifts unto men, imparting the priceless gift of His own righteousness to the helpless human agent. This is the message that God commanded to be given to the world. It is the third angel's message, which is to be proclaimed with a loud voice, and attended with the outpouring of His Spirit in a large measure.[7]

---

1. Letter, May 16, 1916.
2. *The Ellen G. White 1888 Materials,* page 1336.
3. *Review and Herald,* March 5, 1884.
4. Letter, January 9, 1893.
5. *Testimonies to Ministers,* pages 96, 97.
6. *The Ellen G. White 1888 Materials,* page 349.
7. *The Ellen G. White 1888 Materials,* page 1336, 1337.

The Boulder in My Path

I'll admit that I came to my study of the subject of 1888 with a premise. It was based on a passage buried in the *Testimonies*:

> If all who had labored unitedly in the work of 1844 had received the third angel's message and proclaimed it in the power of the Holy Spirit, the Lord would have wrought mightily with their efforts. A flood of light would have been shed upon the world. Years ago the inhabitants of the earth would have been warned, the closing work would have been completed, and Christ would have come for the redemption of His people.[1]

This statement was not something that could be passed over lightly with an "Oh, isn't that nice." It wasn't gift-card poetry, a clever truism, or even an inspiring thought for the day. It was a weighty confrontation saying that Jesus could have come a long time ago (the statement was written in 1893). This notion sat in the middle of my spiritual path like a massive boulder—too heavy to move, too big to climb over, too dark to see through. I had to face it head-on. What it told me was that if a certain message had been received and proclaimed by God's church, the gospel commission would have been completed and the end would have arrived. Serious business.

Oh, I quipped, then *I* never would have existed! The pioneer's mistake is my good fortune! I have human rebellion to thank for my existence.

Fortunately, I snapped out of my narcissism and thought of a few other things that have existed since 1893, such as World War I; World War II; Lenin; Stalin; the Holocaust; the Korean War; Vietnam; Cambodia; Saddam Hussein; Bosnia; Sudan. Each one of these timeline blots represented to my mind millions of lives lived out in veritable torture chambers—futile and pointless, for many ending in unchristian graves. I saw time grinding on, churning out victims of circumstance like so many condemned prisoners numbly marching in the cold. All in the last century. All because of the delay.

Do you get what this means? It's so heavy it snaps the mindscale in two. Something could have prevented all these cataclysms and their respective losses of life. Even more importantly, something could have spared Jesus 100-plus years of empathic suffering. Fearful of oversimplifying a complex issue, knowing how little I knew, I slowly came to the conclusion that the delay was, humanly speaking, preventable.

Ideas like these cause quite a stir. Some say that God's timetable can't be affected by human beings, that to believe otherwise borders on sacrilege. They equate the idea of a waiting Christ with human manipulation of the Divine will—a blasphemous thing indeed. But I feel that inspiration depicts the exact opposite—a God who is in full control of His volitional faculties, but *chooses* to wait until those He loves are ready for Him. This is seen clearly in 2 Peter 3:9: "The Lord is not slow about His promise, as some count slowness, but is patient toward you, not wishing for any to perish but for all to come to repentance."

The logic here is simple. The Lord waits out of patience. It is an exercise in self-restraint, but one born out of tender care. What does He wish to avoid? That "any should perish." What does He wait for? "For all to come to repentance." What is the logical conclusion? That when all come to repentance, the Lord will no longer need to wait. Who are the *all* God is waiting for? Those who will ever respond to the drawing of His Spirit—He knows who they are. The point of all this is that God is waiting for repentance, a divinely-triggered-yet-still-human event, before His second coming, a divine event. This thought is echoed in the writings of God's end-time prophet. "God's unwillingness to have His people perish has been the reason for the so long delay."[2]

As I ruminated on these matters, I thought of the heart of Jesus, open wide to human suffering. I knew that He didn't have the defenses we have against pity, and I saw even the generic suffering all around me through His eyes. A haggard man stood outside my local grocery store with a sign, "WILL WORK FOR FOOD." I wondered about the soul-hunger inside that man, which no food had ever satisfied, which I could not bear to feel, but which Jesus felt as His own. I reflected upon how Jesus felt to the depths the pain of each individual, and I multiplied that pain times 6 billion to get the final product of God's aching heart.

I knew His suffering didn't end at the Cross—I recalled the fact that the cross of Christ was the pinnacle of suffering that continues until now—yes, I knew, Jesus was still suffering because of sin.[3] Every hungry beggar, every abandoned baby, every lonely teenager, every battered wife, every dying elder, was His personal concern. And every act of cruelty He received as if done to Him personally. And yet—according to the Bible—He waits for a response from His end-time people.

Another objection presented itself: Didn't the Father know the time of Jesus' coming? Didn't this mean that He *set* that time? No, I realized, God's foreknowledge does not eclipse human choice. Jesus knew Judas would betray Him, but did He *cause* Judas to betray Him? No, He did everything He could to *prevent* Judas from betraying Him, knowing He would. God can somehow know our choices without consigning us to them.

Biblical proofs began to line themselves up in my mind. I saw that all of the predictions of the Second Advent involved preceding events that involved human beings, namely His church. So many prerequisites to His coming involve a response by human beings that I could not help but reject the "Ready or not, here I come!" model of the Second Advent. I didn't know much, but I knew that before Jesus came:

1. *The gospel would be preached globally.* I recalled the fact that Jesus placed time's cutoff point just after the gospel had been " 'preached in the whole world' " (Matthew 24:14). I knew that the finishing of the gospel commission depended upon the cooperation of human beings, namely His church.

2. *The harvest would ripen.* I found another evidence in the fact that the prepared world is described in prophecy as a "ripe harvest," which

Jesus is told to " 'put in [His] sickle and reap' " (Revelation 14:15). No farmer in his right mind would try to schedule the date of a harvest ahead of time, but would patiently wait until the crop is ready to feel the sharp blade of his reaping tool.

I saw this harvest principle in the parable of the tares, where patience was again enjoined upon the reaper; "allow both [the wheat and the tares] to grow together until the harvest" (Matthew 13:30). This parable applied, I saw, to the end of the world, when "there will be no likeness between good and evil. Then those who have joined the church, but who have not joined Christ, will be manifest."[4] I saw that a human factor, the development and manifestation of character, preceded the harvest.

3. *Christ's character would be manifested.* I thought of the positive aspect of the harvest principle as well. "When the character of Christ shall be perfectly reproduced in His people, then He will come to claim them as His own."[5] I knew that Jesus waited for the manifestation of Himself in His professed followers. He would not return to receive strangers, but familiar friends. One day, I knew, the earth would be separated into two groups—those who knew Him, and those who knew Him not. Those who knew Him would "see Him as He is" (see 1 John 3:2), but those who knew Him not would be destroyed by that same brightness, for "the glory of Him who is love will destroy them."[6] I realized that Jesus delayed His coming because He knew that His glorious love was a consuming fire to the sin-tainted heart. Only when He was sure that sinners were intractable would He venture to unveil His glorious Self. To come before that time would be to destroy what could have been saved.

4. *The sanctuary would be cleansed.* The most solemn truth I had learned as a Seventh-day Adventist was the doctrine of the cleansing of the heavenly sanctuary. The idea that Christ was engaging as High Priest in the work of blotting out of sin had always evoked a certain awe in me, and rightly so. Now I saw that work of cleansing was the culmination of six thousand years of effort on Heaven's part to convince humanity to part with evil. God was faced with two great objectives: to destroy sin and to save sinners. The only way He could do both was to separate them from one another. This was the process that would precede the harvest, and this, the boulder-statement said, would have been greatly catalyzed by a certain message. So catalyzed, in fact, that what has failed to happen in one hundred years could have happened in only a few.

Received, Then Proclaimed

This was an extreme shift in my thinking. I had always believed, perhaps unconsciously, that the Church's unreadiness was the cause of the delay, but I had imbibed, equally unconsciously, of the theory that raising lifestyle standards was the answer. After seeing a few of my champion standard bearers fall, however, I was forced to reassess this thinking. If higher standards were the answer, what would inspire the Church to raise and then keep them? Some motivation beyond what we were currently experiencing must come into play. Boot camp-style reformations would never work. Legislating reforms wouldn't purify God's people any more readily than getting a parrot to recite the Lord's Prayer would make it a Christian.

Maybe the answer was more evangelism. If the Church actually had a job to do before Jesus could return, I mused, we need to get moving (as if we weren't already)! Another crusade, another cell church, another downlink, another radio station were added to the SDA "to do" list.

Now I halted, putting down my brochures to contemplate this boulder-statement that still froze my feet to the ground. I saw that it was not only a passive sin but an *active resistance* that circumvented the "closing work." If we had "received" the third angel's message, as well as "proclaimed it in power," this work would have been finished long ago. Proclamation of the gospel is a sacred duty enjoined upon every one of us, but the most passionate efforts to *proclaim* something we hadn't yet *received* would not achieve the desired result.

I wholeheartedly affirm the sacred call to evangelize, and I feel nothing but joy in seeing the Church grow in numbers. In spite of its imperfections, the Church is the best place to be this side of heaven and is "the one object upon which God bestows in a special sense His supreme regard."[7] But a desire to see souls saved, walks hand in hand with a desire to dry the tears of God. If there is something that stands in the way of His coming, something that prolongs the problem of sin beyond its provident time allotment, won't we who care enough to seek the lost also care to know what that something is?

The proclamation of the gospel to every living soul will follow persecution, when "light will be brought before thousands who otherwise would know nothing of these truths."[8] Persecution is always triggered by the preaching of truth accompanied by a living witness of the gospel.

Many cherish the hope that persecution will be the magic button that arouses Laodicea from her lethargy, but this can't be if the world has no quarrel with a sleeping church. It is a church with a *living* message that rebukes the world into frenzied attempts to suppress it. The more I considered these things, the more I saw that a message received deep into the collective heart of Laodicea would do more to promulgate the gospel than all the man-centered attempts at fulfilling the Great Commission that we could muster.

Haven't we already received it?

Another question came: Hadn't we received the third angel's message already? In 1846 Ellen White had her vision of the heavenly sanctuary in which she saw the Sabbath commandment circled by a halo of light. According to her, this was the beginning of the proclamation of the third angel's message.[9] Still, she claimed in this boulder-statement that the third angel's message had *not* been received and proclaimed in 1893—a seeming contradiction.

I could only conclude that the *heart* of that message was somehow lost in the shuffle of denominational growth over the half century between the time it was first given and the time it was apparently lost. And what was the heart of that message? I recalled her statement: "Several have written to me, inquiring if the message of justification by faith is the third angel's message, and I have answered, 'It is the third angel's message in verity.' "[10] This statement was written in 1890, only two years after the conference when that message was first presented. The evidence was clear—righteousness by faith was, "in verity," the heart of the third angel's message. And in 1888, we lost our heart.

Had it been found since then? The boulder in my path grew larger. If it had been found, received, and proclaimed, then why the tedious droning on of years, now a century of them, since the time when Jesus could have come? Heaven was ready in 1893, humanity wasn't. Heaven had not retracted its bid; humanity was still the hold-up. To conclude otherwise would be to blame God for the previous one hundred years of Divine/human anguish.

I couldn't have proved it to anyone else, but I began to know in my bones that the rejection of the 1888 message lay at the foundation of the delay. The guile of our resistance had caked the sands of time and the hourglass could not run itself out. I knew when I first read the books of Jones and Waggoner, when I first heard the 1888 message taught clearly, that the gospel which was presented there was the heart of Seventh-day Adventism.

Before that, I had seen the doctrines of the Church as separate items on a checklist. I was intimidated by the thought of having to defend my beliefs with my faulty memory and limited knowledge, but the message of righteousness by faith ordered my mind in a way that enabled me to see the truth in its cohesiveness. In the light of the most precious message, I saw the wholeness of present truth and its relationship to the gospel. Jesus, the loving Jesus, the Jesus I had met personally for the first time a decade before as a wayward teenager, this Jesus was at the heart of the message of 1888, and in the light of this Jesus all the intricate doctrines of Adventism made perfect, compassionate sense. My heart was strangely warmed—do I dare admit it?

My purpose is simple. If it is true that this message could have prepared the Church and the world for Christ's coming only a few years after it was given, then we must still be here a century later because that message has not been able to complete its work in us. It is my desire to share within the context of my own fumbling Christian experience something of the transforming power that was promised us so long ago. I saw in the 1888 concepts a powerful dynamic, which still impacts me fifteen years later, and I would like to show it to you. Let's take this journey together.

---

1. *Review and Herald Extra*, Feb. 28, 1893.

2. *Testimonies*, vol. 2, pp. 192, 194.

3. *Education*, p. 263; *"The cross is a revelation to our dull senses of the pain that, from its very inception, sin has brought to the heart of God. Every departure from the right, every deed of cruelty, every failure of humanity to reach His ideal, brings grief to Him."*

4. *Christ's Object Lessons*, p. 74.

5. Ibid., p. 69

6. *Desire of Ages*, p.764.

7. *Acts of the Apostles*, p. 12.

8. *The Great Controversy*, p. 607.

9. *Life Sketches*, pp. 95, 96; *"I was shown that the third angel proclaiming the commandments of God and the faith of Jesus, represents the people who receive this message, and raise the voice of warning to the world to keep the commandments of God and His law as the apple of the eye; and that in response to this warning, many would embrace the Sabbath of the Lord."*

10. *1st Selected Messages*, p. 372.

CHAPTER FOUR

W. D. J. D.?
(What Did Jesus Do?)

It was the fall of 1989. My husband and I had left New Jersey, and I had quit my job in Manhattan when we discovered I was pregnant with baby number one. We rented a small solar house for ourselves in the middle of a huge dandelion field in southern Massachusetts. Not too long after, a little sister was born. We were so fortunate, so blessed, to have two healthy children, an intact family, and food on the table.

But there were problems. At thirty-one I developed allergies. Not just allergies to a few foods, but to every food. Not just to pollen in the spring, but to everything that suspended itself in the air, from mold spores to dust mite feces. I was tired and lethargic, and worst of all, my entire respiratory tract swelled.

This is not a big deal for most, but I was a singer. Slowly it dawned upon me that my pipes were suffering. The tone wasn't as clear. The pitch wasn't as perfect. The volume wasn't as strong. I still had songs inside of me, but the more I tried to make my swollen vocal chords coordinate their movements to express those musical thoughts, the more frustrated I became. My songwriting and singing had been my "contribution" and a source of self-worth, and now I was losing my career, my health, and my ministry in one package. I started to panic.

I sought the help of doctors, who prescribed medicines that helped slightly but made me tired, and I was even worse off the day after I took them. I began to get respiratory infections, which required more medications for treatment; medications I loathed and needed at the same time. One doctor thought sinus surgery might be the answer, so I had one, then two, and in the end four sinus surgeries.

I became a favorite of every multi-level marketing supplement sales person who descended upon me like ants on a picnic. The blue-green, fiber-filled, enzyme-rich, phyto-blast concoctions without exception came guaranteed to cure me and, without exception, didn't. I tried strict diets and elimination diets, mono diets, fasting, hydrotherapy, and massage. Last but not least, I tried prayer. Nothing helped. Nothing.

When the realization that my condition was chronic hit me, it was as if black clouds had rolled into the sky. "Why me?" I demanded of God when I could bring myself to speak to Him. I took walks in the forest and fields while my children were napping and begged Him to tell me why He chose a singer instead of someone who wouldn't have been so devastated. The sky stared back as silent as stone. From this point I began to feel, not to think, but to feel, that God had abandoned me.

Once that feeling settled, it was as hard to shake as a bloodsucker. Oh, I carried on—functioned because I had to, loved my children because they needed it, smiled because the world diden't have enough smiles, but I was plagued inside. The toughest thing about this was that nothing of religion seemed to help.

Pat phrases like "trust God" fell as dead leaves to the ground.

Sermons clattered like empty offering plates.

Caring words sounded sarcastic.

Boy, was I bummed out!

I think they call it depression. It's when all the worst dreads that you house in your unconscious come flying up like bats out of hell. You can't see anything but the chaos of your own negativity, and you can't trust anyone to help you even though you are helpless to fight it alone.

Normal depression is brought on by circumstances, but in susceptible people a short-term bout of depression can lead into chronic depression that continues long after the circumstances have stabilized. This was the danger I was in when my voice failed. For the first time in my twelve-year-old Christian experience I began to question God, and since my entire life was centered on religion this was kind of an awkward thing to do.

Fortunately, I had begun to understand the gospel more clearly, and frankly, it saved the day. No, it didn't instantly remove all suffering and launch me into a state of ecstasy, but it did give me the tools necessary to process a major life crisis. I don't think that the previous conception I had of life, love, and God would have been adequate to catch me in my descent as I felt the claws of despair and the urges of suicide. But "God is faithful, who will not allow you to be tempted beyond what you are able, but with the temptation will also make the way of escape, that you may be able to bear it" (1 Corinthians 10:13, NKJV). He allowed the "message of His healing grace"[1] to come into my life when the healing was the most desperately needed. I probably wouldn't have paid attention otherwise.

The purpose of the following chapters is to try to convey that understanding of the gospel in the context of my own life. My study of the 1888 message was like an open gate into a beautiful field of revelation: No, not an end, but a beginning with an end in sight. Jones and Waggoner were given a message that was to be "the *beginning* of the light of the angel whose glory shall fill the whole earth"[2] (emphasis mine). It was like the sketch on a canvas waiting for the paint—more would come, but what was there was essential. For me it was the beginning of my tapping into deeper motives and truths than I ever had before.

Where I Am

When someone is ill or discouraged, the typical human response is to avoid him or her. If you aren't convinced of this, become ill or discouraged, then count your friends. You may only need one finger—for Jesus.

There were a few souls brave enough to meet me in my dark valley, but it was usually to blurt out a few platitudes, pray as if they were warding off evil spirits, tell me to snap out of it, and then flee. As never before I sensed how incapable most humans are to enter into the pain of another. But God be praised, the loneliness of this realization only made the truths I was learning more welcome.

As I studied, I realized that God's response to human suffering was the opposite of the typical human response. In short, God drew near when people drew back. One of the most prominent thoughts in all of Jones and Waggoner's teaching was the nearness of the Savior. As Jones put it, Jesus "has come to us just where we are." He prefaces this thought with:

The idea of the natural mind (is) that God is too pure and too holy to dwell with us and in us in our sinful human nature; that sinful as we are, we are too far off for Him in His purity and holiness to come to us just where we are.[3]

Our damaged natures make certain ones of us prone to become depressed. I was grateful to be reminded that Jesus actually experienced feelings of depression at different points in His life, especially Gethsemane and Calvary. He did not succumb to depression as I had, but He empathized with me in that He knew what I was up against. Because He came near and faced my temptations, I could trust Him to lead me out of them.

A whole new understanding of Christ's humanity opened up to me. I had always been so afraid of the topic because of the contention that surrounded it, but now the Bible verses that seemed beyond me became clear. I saw that Jesus took upon Himself my fallen, frail flesh with all my genetic weaknesses and liabilities that He could be two things—my Savior and my Example.

My Savior—"What Did Jesus Do?"

Something that has helped me grasp all that Jesus did as our Savior from sin is to divide the sin problem into three "P's": penalty, power, and presence. The Bible is very clear that a debt was incurred because of sin, and this may be thought of as sin's *penalty*. It is also clear that sin has an addictive and destructive *power*. Finally, we live in a world full of sorrow and temptations, and in frail, fallen flesh, and so we ultimately need salvation from the *presence* of sin. Delivery from sin, therefore, comes in three phases: delivery from the penalty of sin comes at the Cross; delivery from the power of sin comes when we *receive* the atonement; and delivery from the presence of sin will come when the Crucified One returns as King.

At the Fall, the foremost threat to our existence was the penalty of sin, which was death. Even if we could somehow escape from the *power* and *presence* of sin without God's intervention, we would still owe our blood because of the legal debt that sin incurred. Jesus answered to this debt with His own blood, His human blood in which the life streams of all of humanity flowed. That blood was precious, something of exorbitant value, because it was also God's blood. Thus, the blood of Christ bridged the gap between humanity and Divinity; it flowed from our elder brother, a member of our condemned race, and it also came from the veins of One who was as holy as the law itself.

Oh, how valuable that blood was, and how little we comprehend it! It bought back the human family from the dominion of darkness, and in so doing, obliterated any right that kingdom has over us! We are no longer debtors to the flesh (see Romans 8:12) because Jesus "shared in the same" flesh and blood so that "through death He might destroy him who had the power of death, that is, the devil, and release those who through fear of death were all their lifetime subject to bondage" (Hebrews 2:14, 15, NKJV). "For the death that He died, He died to sin, once for all" (Romans 6:10). The result was freedom, release from bondage, because "he who has died is freed from sin" (v. 7).

What I am saying is that Jesus qualified Himself to be our Substitute by assuming human nature and dying as us. This is why Christ's human nature is "everything to us."[4] God's justice hinges upon it. If Jesus had died as One unconnected to humanity, then His dying in place of me would have been unjust. Let me explain further.

The law of God, and the laws of all civilized governments, demands the price of a crime to be paid by the *very one* who commits it. " 'The soul who sins shall die. The son shall not bear the guilt of the father, nor the father bear the guilt of the son' " (Ezekiel 18:20, NKJV). For a government to let one die in place of another would be evidence that it was highly corrupt.

Can you imagine reading the headlines one morning and finding that an innocent child volunteered to die in the electric chair in place of a serial killer? You would be impressed with the self-sacrifice of the child, but equally, if not more, aghast at the corruption of the government that allowed such a compromise of justice! In the same way, a version of substitution that sees Jesus dying purely *in place* of me, without an intimate connection *to* me, conveys a form of injustice.

But this could not be said of God's government in accepting the sacrifice of Jesus, because He didn't die merely as a separate individual, He died as my Representative, having qualified Himself for that position by clothing His divinity with my fallen humanity. "By sending His own Son in the likeness of sinful flesh, on account of sin: He condemned sin in the flesh" (Romans 8:3, NKJV). Jesus performed the feat of condemning *sin* without condemning *sinners* by becoming one with me and dying my death as His own.

But Jesus didn't only receive the penalty of sin in fallen flesh, He took humanity through the dark passage of the grave to new life when He was raised in glorified form. Because He had lived a sinless life, the grave had no right to hold Him. Jesus said, " 'the ruler of this world is coming, and *he has nothing in Me*' " (John 14:30, emphasis mine), and " 'I lay down My life that I may take it again' " (John 10:17). I was captive to the grave, but when Jesus " 'ascended on high, He led captivity captive,' " (Ephesians 4:8, NKJV). Now I am captive to the hope of everlasting life.

Imagine God's boldness! He saved me from the condemnation of sin whether I wanted Him to or not. He didn't send a consent form, or phone me for an authorization, but now that the foundation of my salvation is complete, it is God's hope and deep desire that I will build upon it by His grace. As I come to understand what Jesus accomplished *without* my cooperation, I am ready to believe what He can accomplish *with* my cooperation.

I vividly recall one beautiful Mother's Day that came in the midst of my worst depression. Spring was coming on full bore. Everything was beautiful to the eye but the pollen was also thick in the air. I stared out my window feeling incredibly sorry for myself and moaning, "Happy Mother's Day." What a sad-sack!

If you had told me right then that depression was a sin that I needed to overcome, I might have spit in your face. But over the next years the gospel dawned upon my soul in such a fashion that I *wanted* to be done with my self-will and give Him complete rights of occupancy in my heart. How did it happen? I was so moved by the complete work that Christ accomplished *for* me that I desired Him to accomplish a complete work *in* me.

The sanctification process is actually a joyful journey if the gospel is in place in our thinking. But if the idea of overcoming has at times been a choke-chain around your neck, you're not alone at all. Still, there is hope that it will become a flight of freedom. Let me tell you how it has worked for me.

The Buyer and the Bought

Against the deep black of his skin his teeth were white as chalk
Crying out indignant from the auction block

And though they tried to shut him down the angry words came
through
"Don't buy me, I won't work for you!"

"Don't say a word!" the auctioneer yelled straight into his face
Then turned to sell his fellow at a fiendish pace
And still the slave did murmur of the thing he'd never do
"Don't buy me, I won't work for you!"

Now, one man bid a handsome price the others worked around
But every time they countered, he would bid them down
At last the slave belonged to him who heard the oath anew
"Don't buy me, I won't work for you!"

Out to the fields the two men walked, the buyer and the bought
The free man walked in silence while the bound man fought
"You've wasted all your money, sir," the slave cried, "I warned you,"
"Don't buy me, I won't work for you!"

So, two men stood there face to face as time seemed to stand still
The slave grew almost silent, but unrelenting still
His hateful words hung in the air, so soon to be untrue
"Don't buy me, I won't work for you!"

The slave's new owner took his prize, the shackles and the key
And to the slave's amazement, set his prisoner free
The slave fell down on ragged knees, the broken words came through,
"You've bought me, I'll do anything for you."

So, maybe all this stubborn pride we tend to throw around
Is just conclusive proof that we believe we're bound
And if we just believe we're free, we'll say, "What can I do?"
Freed slaves say, "I'll do anything for you."

_____

1. *The Ellen G. White 1888 Materials,* page 409.
2. *The Ellen G. White 1888 Materials,* page 1073.
3. Jones, A. T., *The Consecrated Way,* page 31.

CHAPTER FIVE

W. W. J. D.?
(What Would Jesus Do?)

Our family attended a church pastored by a close friend of many years named Steven. One day Pastor Steven handed me a paper and asked me to fill it out for a stress seminar he was going to conduct. Participants were to be rated ahead of time according to their stress level so that he would know just what he was dealing with in trying to help them. Divorce, house fires, bankruptcy, death; these were all events that shot the general stress level up.

My questionnaire scored so high that I compared with people who had experienced major disasters. (OK, OK, I'm a little high-strung to begin with, but the health and career problems I was having were serious, and I was glad someone finally acknowledged them, even if it was only a bunch of emotionally contracted research scientists who didn't care whether I lived or died.)

"Your questionnaire really concerned me, Jennifer," Steven said with a puzzled look on his face.

"Well, I'm really messed up, I told you that. Now that it's on paper, you believe me," I jabbed.

"Well, what can we do to help you?" he asked in total sincerity.

I was stumped. "I don't know. When I'm at church I feel like I have to put on a front so as not to burden anyone."

The pastor knew the right answer. "Well, don't put on a front, stand up and ask people to pray for you."

I couldn't. "I'm afraid I'll turn into a demoniac the minute I start talking!" I cried.

That didn't faze him. He said, "Well, go ahead and be a demoniac!"

I was stunned. Imagine a pastor giving me permission to impinge upon the precious tranquility of his worship service so that I could vent my bottled up emotions! The feeling of actually having a safety net, having permission to be where I was at that moment and still be accepted, freed me.

This is exactly how the gospel works. If the pressure to perform eclipses the fact that Christ died for us when our performance stunk, we will in the end fail to perform. Amazingly, if we turn the priorities around and sink our hearts into the good news of what God has *already* done for us, we will *want* to "perform" for His sake.

Here it is in more theological terms: To present Jesus as Example without first presenting Him as Savior is almost a form of cruelty, because it holds the duty of righteous living before us without first providing the motivation of good news. "What would Jesus do?" should come after "What *did* Jesus do?" Once we truly comprehend and appreciate what Jesus accomplished for us, we will eagerly ask what we might accomplish for Him.

Until we have the proper motivation in place, standards do serve one valid purpose—to awaken us to our need of Christ. If our need is not met with the revelation of God's saving grace, however, the preaching of standards becomes destructive. If the example of Jesus is upheld without the saving grace of Jesus receiving all the more attention, we will inevitably feel the condemnation of the law.

There are two human methods of coping with condemnation: despair and denial. Most people are too weak-willed and lacking in self-confidence to fool themselves into believing they can make it on their own, and they despair. A few stalwarts can manufacture a good enough appearance to convince everyone, including themselves, that they can make the grade, and they deny their true condition. I have been in groups where standards were touted in the absence of the true joy of the gospel, and it was just this way—there were a few standard-bearers with their noses in the air, and a majority of despondent ones with their faces to the ground. Experience has taught me that without a clear answer to the question, "What *did* Jesus do?" we will either live in self-deception or selfish insecurity.

With a foundation of the gospel, however, we can accept the fact that Jesus is our Example in freedom from the mastery of sin. Jesus first points us to what He has accomplished *for* us and *as* us, then informs us of what He will accomplish *in* us. At the point in my journey when I realized this principle, I saw a pattern in many scriptures that looked like this:

1. You are set free from the condemnation of sin.
2. You are set free from sin itself.

Jesus' words to the woman taken in adultery were:
1. "Neither do I condemn you" (you are set free from the condemnation of sin).
2. "Go and sin no more" (you are set free from sin itself—see John 8:11).

His words to us in Romans 8:3 and 4 (NKJV) are similar:
1. "He condemned sin in the flesh" (you are set free from the condemnation of sin).
2. "That the righteous requirement of the law might be fulfilled in us who do not walk according to the flesh but according to the Spirit" (you are set free from sin itself).

Lest we think this is a purely New Testament concept, let's look at the Ten Commandments in Exodus 20:
1. "I am the Lord your God who brought you out of the land of Egypt, out of the house of bondage" (you are set free from the condemnation of sin).
2. "You shall have no other gods before me, etc . . ." (these are not stifling restraints but promises telling us that we are set free from sin itself!).

Once I recognized this pattern, I saw it everywhere. Many of the letters of Paul, for instance, start out with an explanation of what God has already done for all of humanity in Christ. Then they talk about receiving His righteousness, and finally, they address standards of Christian living.

Fashionable Sins?

While it is cruel to browbeat people with high standards without first establishing the gospel, it is equally cruel to tell them there is no overcoming sin at all. The fact that we have been given power to walk without falling is good news if we truly hate the sin that caused our Jesus to be crucified. Sin brings misery to those who commit it, and that misery bleeds out to others. Why spread misery when we don't have to? Practically speaking, we may fall even as consecrated Christians, but our attitude toward sin is changed.

It is harder for some of us to feel urgent about our "little white sins" because they are not of a socially abhorrent character. Some of us can live reasonably productive and happy lives even though we remain bound to various infractions and never truly conquer self-will. Others, however, have besetting sins that bring them ostracism and shame. If we believe that it is impossible to overcome sin, what comment do we make to such ones?

Take my friend Tom, for instance. He was violently raped and molested as a young boy. As is too often the case, the psychological changes that result from traumas like this are such that the person sometimes repeats history and goes on to do to others what was done to them. Tom became a pedophile. When he came to our local church he was a convicted felon with victims strewn all over the country. We could say in truth that Tom's besetting sin was child molestation. For me to preach that sin could not possibly be overcome would be to tell Tom that he couldn't be expected to stop abusing.

On the other hand, if I were to tell him that his sin of molestation must be overcome, but my sin of losing my temper was OK, I would be guilty of holding up a double standard. This double standard results in social divisions within the body of Christ. It was the same in Jesus' day—there were people with fashionable sins like self-righteousness and pride, and those with "really bad" sins like tax collecting and harlotry. Jesus came to sweep away the false divisions by showing that there are no fashionable sins with God and that all are capable of the worst sin.

In fact, in my temper problem (OK, I do have one, but I am willing and God is able), I am showing an essential disposition to forgo the presence of Christ in my life in exchange for a moment of indulgence, just as Tom does when he abuses. For me the indulgence is rage-venting, which brings no legal consequences, but for him the indulgence is perversity, which will land him in jail and damage another young life like his was damaged.[3]

An essential feature of being set free from sin is the return of free choice. We had no such thing when we were slaves of sin, but through His life and death Jesus broke the power that sin exerts over us, and in so doing gave us back our will to choose. "Knowing this, that our old man was crucified with Him, that the body of sin might be done away with, that we should no longer be slaves of sin" (Romans 6:6, NKJV).

"Our old man" was our fallen nature enclosed in His. Since we were crucified with Him, sin has lost its right to rule over us. When we were owned by the kingdom of darkness, Satan held our wills captive, for he is a god of coercion. Now that we have been bought back by the kingdom of light, Christ set our wills free, even to choose sin, for He is the God of liberty.

Now, because of the gospel, sin may become an act of the will. While built into our natures and our surroundings are enticements to sin, the ultimate decision to act upon those provocations is volitional. In assuming our fallen humanity without participating in our sin, Jesus insured for all time that sin could be a matter of choice and not necessity.

Although His temptations were greater than ours, this fact is inclusive rather than exclusive. Jesus was tempted to use His divine power to extricate Himself from the cross, and we have no such temptation, but for Him to follow the plan of God in going to the cross required submission of His will to God. In this the greatest-of-all-temptations, the essential elements of every temptation converged—self-will versus God's will. When Jesus faced temptation in this ultimate form, it encompassed, rather than excluded, our smaller temptations. I have no trouble believing that "He was tempted in all points like as we are, yet without sin," when I recognize that He battled with Self, as I must. He said, "Not my will, but Thine be done." If He could resist the severe temptation to assert His divinity when facing the loss of all He cherished, then why couldn't He by the same token face the lesser temptations that we are beleaguered by and be likewise the Overcomer?

Jesus does not ask us to do the impossible. On what basis could He say to the woman taken in adultery, "Go and sin no more," and to His people, "sin not," (see John 8:11 and 1 John 2:1) if it was not possible to obey Him? For Him to advocate abstinence from sin at all, whether as a lifestyle or an occasional slip-up, would have been heartless if He had not first overcome with the same or greater challenges than we have.

Yet speaking practically, we do sin. Often! How do we resolve the tension between the possibility of overcoming and the reality that we haven't yet? We submit ourselves to Him even in this: that in His time and way we will have deliverance. Until then, we fix our eyes on Jesus and "press on toward the goal for the prize of the upward call of God in Christ Jesus" (Philippians 3:14).

Like the babe attempting her first toddles, we look full in the face of Jesus, eager to please, bathing in His affirmation. If we fall, we rise again and walk toward the One behind that flashing camera. Does Jesus despise our falls? No more than the happy parent of a baby learning to walk. Does the babe stop trying because there is no condemnation when she fails? No, she enjoys Mom and Dad's happiness far, far too much.

The Masterpiece
If there were no shadows
There would be no shade
And if there were no helpless
There would be no aid
And if there were no wanderers
There would be no prayer
And if there were no dying
There would be no care

If there were no orphans
Would adoption be?
And if there were no prisoners
None would be set free
And if there were no prodigals
How could Father show
What it is to love someone
Who doesn't even know?

All you hopeless children
All you dying ones
All you orphan daughters

Prodigal sons
There's no restoration
Where there is no loss
Take this grand occasion
To embrace the cross
It's when all is broken
And you're on your knees
That from broken pieces
Comes the masterpiece

---

1. White, Ellen, *The Youth's Instructor,* Oct. 13, 1898.
2. Waggoner, E. J., *Christ and His Righteousness,* page 114.
3. *Please don't think that I am putting all sin on an equality in every context. Church discipline is a necessary and healthy directive and requires differentiating between sin worthy of disciplinary action and sin not worthy. I have heard too many abusers ask self-righteously, "Do you ever break the speed limit?" Let's use three things when dealing with sin in the context of church membership: love, biblical guidelines, and common sense.*

CHAPTER SIX

You
Be the Judge

My friend Trina* and I had a two-women mutual admiration society. Both singer/songwriters, we swapped songs, shared producers and sang background vocals for each other on a regular basis. She thought I was a great songwriter, once even crying while I played her a new song. "I'm not crying because the song was sad," she sniffed, "but because I didn't write it!" My admiration for Trina was mutual. She was a winner of a girl with her good looks, gorgeous voice, and bubbly personality, and I knew her ministry would blossom.

Hundreds of people were disappointed when Trina chose to leave the Seventh-day Adventist Church. She wrote a letter informing us that she had asked that her name be removed from the books. She listed the reasons carefully, which included a loss of confidence in the idea of the investigative judgement, Adventist interpretation of prophecy, the prophetic calling of Ellen White, and the Sabbath as a sign of God's people in the end times. As I studied her letter and the booklet she sent along with it, I realized that the central point of controversy was the doctrine of the cleansing of the heavenly sanctuary.

This doctrine is the only teaching that is completely singular to Seventh-day Adventism. It is, in that sense, our right to exist as a denomination. Other churches embrace Sabbath keeping, some agree with our view of the state of man in death. Many churches advocate tithe paying and most are preaching some version of the health message. Truly the doctrine of the cleansing of the sanctuary is Adventism's unique contribution.

A brief explanation of our view is this: The sanctuary Moses built was patterned after the great sanctuary in heaven where Christ is now acting as High Priest. This means that, like the earthly sanctuary, the heavenly had two compartments; one where forgiveness took place and one where final cleansing took place. The Church was founded on the discovery that Jesus has been in the "cleansing phase" of His ministry since 1844, and that He will eventually remove all the compiled sin from the sanctuary, as in the ancient Day of Atonement. We teach that He will then place it on the head of Satan, symbolized by the scapegoat in Leviticus 16. It is easy to reason that in order for Christ to cleanse the sanctuary, there must be an end to the "inflowing" of sin, or its cleansing would be futile. This has traditionally been recognized by some as a call to sinless living.

All of the above is rejected by my friend Trina and her teachers, and some even within Adventism today. No doubt this is, in some cases, because of the legalism that has often accompanied its teaching. But does this view *automatically* lead to an eclipsing of the gospel and insecurity in regards to salvation? I think not, if it is taught in the light of righteousness by faith. In fact, as I became acquainted with the concepts of the 1888 message, I saw how its reception would have prevented much confusion among us today in regards to the sanctuary truth. This is what I hope to share in the next few pages.

Fight or Flight Reaction

As a convert to Adventism, I had sought long and hard for the truths that the Church holds. When I first learned about the ministry of Christ in the sanctuary in heaven, I felt like my shovel had struck gold. My newly converted heart wanted to know where my Jesus was and what He was doing, and as I studied Adventist beliefs, that inquiry was answered satisfactorily for the first time. I relished the teaching of the heavenly ministry of Christ like a thirsty traveler gulps water.

But over the years, I witnessed applications of the belief that were twisted into a fear-driven doctrine that deluded some and discouraged others. I have known people who preached that, since we are living in the end times, sinlessness is required for salvation. The thinking behind such teaching goes like this: Since Christ's ministry is in the cleansing phase, and the cases of the living are being judged, we are in constant danger of being caught with unforgiven sin on our record. The only hope of salvation, then (according to this thinking), is to be sinless.

I saw this focus produce strange, unnatural results. Friends seemed to live in fear of sinning, observing their religious and lifestyle rituals as if their lives depended on them. Not a few of these turned away from the Church entirely, burned out and gospel-hardened.

I realize now that my own reaction to this fear mentality was to develop an eating disorder. I felt that if I could just keep myself weak and innocuous I might keep from sinning. Dietary deprivation was a form of soul purging for me, which, I hoped, would result in purification. I was like one of the self-starving saints of the Middle Ages, seeking holiness of mind through the affliction of the body. Others around me developed different compulsions, but we all had one thing in common: a security blanket that kept us from losing our souls.

This was fear-based, "fight-or-flight" religion. It was fueled by the adrenaline surge that we feel when faced with danger. This is a God-given emergency reaction that beefs up our physical strength so that we can attack (fight) or run from (flight) our enemies. The phenomenon comes in handy in a danger-filled world, but if it is drawn upon for a prolonged period of time, the mechanism itself becomes a threat to our safety. Constant stress and fear wear out the life forces and eventually bring total collapse. This is why so many of my perfectionistic friends finally gave up on religion—they had something akin to adrenal gland fatigue.

The real tragedy of this approach to religion is that the perceived enemy, the one that triggers fight-or-flight, is God. I believe in a proper fear of God, but I see that when that fear is maintained for long periods without maturing into reverential love, the result is spiritual breakdown. This is why the doctrine of eternally burning hell is so insidious—it produces "millions of skeptics and infidels."[1] In the same way, the fear-based perversion of the investigative judgement has led many to reject the idea entirely.

Is it possible to teach something as serious as the cleansing of the heavenly sanctuary and the judgement of the living without catapulting believers into a fear mode? Yes, if this doctrine is presented in the light of God's desire to save us. One of the great tasks of the message of 1888 was to put these teachings within the context of the gospel. Once the gospel motivations were in place, these "frightening" doctrines took on a whole different tone—no less solemn, but characterized by joy in Christ, rather than fear of being out of Christ. I realized as I studied that it was not God's intention to spook anyone into obedience or to trick anyone out of salvation, but rather, through these doctrines, to cement their commitment to Him and reinforce their conviction that He is love.

A Bigger Picture

There is no denying that the putting away of sin is intrinsic to a belief in the investigative judgement, and that this has traditionally produced legalism in our midst. Here is where this teaching goes awry for many: While we focus on our own need to overcome, we are bound to become self-absorbed. When we attempt to live sinlessly in order to achieve spiritual security or a good self-image, our efforts to overcome are completely futile because the root of sin, which is selfishness, is still alive and kicking within us.

This problem is solved, however, when we look at the putting away of sin in relationship to others rather than ourselves. There is something much bigger than our own salvation and happiness at stake. We see sin in the context of the great controversy, realizing that it is our love of sin that keeps Jesus from returning. The unique doctrine of the cleansing of the sanctuary, rather than imprisoning us to selfish motives, *delivers* us from them by putting sin in a larger context than our own lives. It moves our focus from our own navels to the big picture of the cosmic conflict.

Now, the putting away of sin changes color in two ways:

Change number one. The focus shifts from me to Christ. No longer are my attempts to overcome a self-purging penance, but a love-motivated desire to cooperate with Christ in the sacred work He is performing in heaven. This involves me developing a security that is based, not on my own personal status before God, but upon the larger issue of *His* status before the universe.

From its alpha, the great controversy has been over the character of God, which went on trial before the universe with Lucifer's first lies. The cleansing of the sanctuary marks the end of that 6,000-year discord, culminating in the battle between the beast-power and the Lamb, where the character of good will be fully displayed alongside the character of evil. Those who witness this revelation will be so thoroughly convinced of God's love that they will be able to say, " 'Great and marvelous are Your works, Lord God Almighty! Just and true are Your ways, O King of the saints!' " (Revelation 15:3, NKJV). This is called the "song of Moses and the Lamb."

It is highly significant that both Moses and Christ were willing to lay down their own salvation in order to secure the salvation of others, and in so doing, exalt the name or reputation of God. (See Exodus 32:32 and 2 Corinthians 5:21.) Their obsession was not over their place in the kingdom, but over the exaltation of the kingdom itself. This is the bottom line of the security that is derived from an unshakable confidence in God's love—our priority is that others see what we have seen of His goodness. Which brings me to—

Change number two. The focus shifts from me to the *body* of Christ. This is a "group effort" in that the focus is not upon the individual, but upon the collective body. The Bible does not admonish us to overcome as individuals for our own sake, but as a body for Christ's sake. This is powerful prevention for the separatist brand of perfectionism that leads people to fear being "tainted" by fellowship with the local church because it is filled with "Babylon." We are only as good as our relationship to the body, not saved in groups, but grown in relationship to one another.

The depth of our commitment to "The Head," Jesus Christ, is reflected in, and often tested by, our love for "The Body," His church. Jesus will lead us "till we *all* come to the unity of the faith and of the knowledge of the Son of God, to a perfect man, to the measure of the stature of the fullness of Christ" (Ephesians 4:13, NKJV, emphasis mine). Notice from this that "we all" in "unity" produce "a perfect man."

This focus on the ministry of Christ in the sanctuary, if presented in the light of the gospel, has the effect of *releasing* me from self-centeredness as I foster a "team spirit" and an "others centered" approach to the putting away of sin. My sin affects others, I see, and it affects God. Overcoming is no longer about achieving security for myself, it is about working with God toward the "eternal basis of security." [2] He wants to place all things upon the manifestation of His character alongside the manifestation of the character of evil. What a relief to be released from pathetic self-concern to the freedom of sinking my heart into the grand issues of the great controversy! What a privilege to be able to play a tiny part in something so much bigger than myself.

The investigative judgment proves God's goodness, not our own. It showcases His power in human lives. Heaven and earth wait to see whether God's love can transform humanity back into His image. "For the earnest expectation of the creation eagerly waits for the revealing of the sons of God" (Romans 8:19, NKJV). The toughest "road test" for God's grace has been the narcissistic human heart. Can even *that* test be passed? The final cleansing of the sanctuary in heaven says it can.

To worry about my individual salvation in the time of the investigative judgment is like someone on a sinking ship trying to swim to safety from the middle of the ocean—their time would be better spent keeping the ship afloat. (Not merely because their survival was bound up in the survival of the ark of safety, but because the survival of the ship means the survival of many.) Ultimately the Body's corporate desire to see the character of God vindicated will totally eclipse self-concern. The end-time believers fear that they have unconfessed sins, not because it would cause them to be lost, but because "God's holy name would be reproached."[3] This turning away from obsessing over my individual salvation to the "salvation" of the cause of God will result in the most "saved" people who have ever lived in that they have been entirely delivered from the root of sin itself.

The unique doctrine of the cleansing of the sanctuary has not imprisoned me in fear, but delivered me from it. Paradoxically, it has done so by leading me to a higher motive than my own security. True security in Christ is like a butterfly, the more you chase it, the more it eludes you. How much better to make our security His concern, and His vindication in the earth our concern. I believe God has given us a message that will accomplish just that.

Love motivation asks what Jesus is doing today.
Self-motivation is indifferent or afraid to find out.

Love motivation grows out of a solemn reverence for God.
Self-motivation is either irreverent or afraid of God.

Love motivation sees the sin problem in relation to God and others.
Self-motivation sees the sin problem only in relation to me.

Love motivation seeks to put away sin in joyful cooperation with the work Christ is doing in the heavenly sanctuary.

Self-motivation seeks to put away sin in *fear* of the work Christ is doing in the heavenly sanctuary.

Love motivation leads to a growing relationship to the Body of Christ, that a corporate demonstration of the goodness of God might be made.

Self-motivation leads to a rejection of the Body of Christ, that the individual might not be tainted by the sins of the church.

Love motivation joyfully accepts the investigative judgment, knowing that God is ultimately the one being judged.

Self-motivation woefully dreads the investigative judgment, thinking that I am ultimately the one being judged.

---

* Trina is a pseudonym.

1. *The Great Controversy,* page 536.

2. Ibid., page 759; *"It was God's purpose to place things on an eternal basis of security, and in the councils of heaven it was decided that time must be given for Satan to develop the principles which were the foundation of his system of government."*

3. Ibid., page 619.

CHAPTER SEVEN

Love: What's Your Definition?

The clerk at Wurlitzer's music store was either selling me a product or himself, I couldn't tell which. He was one of those people who wore their emotions on the outside rather than tucking them neatly inside like most of us do. "Tion" was his name, pronounced "Shawn," but of course he couldn't spell it in a conventional way, lest his radical persona be somehow tamed. I had made a passing comment to the clerk standing next to him about how I loved the music of "The Messiah," and Tion literally exploded with rage.

"Oh, those farcical cads!" he yelled, "those classical composers were all the same. They write all this music about *God,* and they were all going to prostitutes, or they were *sons* of prostitutes, or they were hoping to *be* prostitutes . . . ."

I was amused and rattled simultaneously. "What kind of music do you do?" I asked politely, knowing that he was a musician because all the guys at Wurlitzer's had a band they were hoping would become the next big rock-and-roll phenomenon.

"Heavy metal," he said, then added in a solemn tone, "heavy, *heavy* metal. What kind do you do?"

"I'm a songwriter, I guess you could say kind of a folk style, and my music is all Christian," I said.

"You're a *Christian*?" he almost shouted, "I can't believe you buy that stuff! Hey, I have a deal I make with Christians! I'll take you out to dinner and pay for everything—the food, the dessert, the coffee, *everything* if you will convince me that the Bible is true."

I immediately thought of two questions. One—was the "deal with Christians" with only young female Christians or any Christian? Two—provided I could find a chaperone, did I have to convince him that the Bible was true *before* or *after* he took me out to dinner?

Ah, forget it, I thought. The point is that this kid is searching, and he's reaching out to the unknown, i. e. connection with God, through the known, i. e. flirting with every woman who will talk to him.

"Well, Tion, let me think about that," I said, wondering how I was going to pull this off. He wrapped up the machine I had bought and we chatted for a few more minutes, him doing most of the talking about the band he played with, the drugs he took, and how he loved the Jewish qabbalah (ka-ba-lah). At one point, he pulled out his tattered paperback copy and let me browse it for a few minutes.

"You like reading this stuff?" I asked, boggle-minded.

"Yeah, it makes sense to me," he said, "but you can try to sell me on Christianity if you want. I'm not kidding! I'll pay for everything, the food, the dessert, the coffee . . ."

"I don't drink coffee," I said, "Can I bring someone with me?"

Tion agreed to a third party and I informed him that we wouldn't expect him to pay. The date was set, and the third party was my pastor, someone I thought would be able to help me meet Tion's mind.

But it wasn't about meeting a mind, it was about winning a heart, and Tion's heart wasn't ready to be won. Somehow I felt an affinity for this kid, though, and we continued to be friendly for several months. I discovered that Tion had a wife and child that he was separated from and that he was planning a divorce.

Then one day Tion disappeared with a newfound girlfriend. He never came into Wurlitzer's, never told a soul. He just vanished. The manager at Wurlitzer's gave me the phone number of his abandoned wife, who I called with the intuition that I could somehow help her. I invited her to my home and she actually agreed to come, not knowing me from Eve.

Rebecca turned out to be a beautiful young dark-haired girl with a son named "Zac," who was Tion's red-haired replica. Within a few minutes of entering my house she was weeping uncontrollably. She had really loved the guy—the farcical cad, to be exact—and now she was living with his ghost in the form of her son. Over the next month I befriended her, brought her groceries, and told her about the Lord. I think she'll make it, but I know he *never* will. Not without a change.

My encounter with Tion was during the season of my life that I was grappling with depression. His wild spirit brought back memories of a time before my Christian conversion when I was similarly steered by impulses and passions. Now I was a mother at home with two small children, a fragmented dream of being a musician, and a big "Why, God?" question hanging in my head. As much as I was witnessing to Tion, he was witnessing to me about a life of unfettered self-expression and escapism. Just when my own life seemed futile he reminded me of a reckless option that was almost tantalizing. Then the product of his recklessness walked through my door in the form of Rebecca and Zac and I knew I could never take that option.

In Tion I saw the issues of love from a point close enough to feel them but detached enough to analyze them. He was bored with his marriage and felt suffocated by commitment, so he bowed out and went in search of the next conquest. Self-fulfillment and morality were at sword's point in his life, and self-fulfillment won out. There is no point in harping on the fact that he will never have lasting self-fulfillment *without* morality. He was too short-sighted to forgo momentary gratification for long-term gratification. And even for those of us with enough self-discipline to delay gratification in order to prolong it, the motive is still self-centered. How would it be for a husband to say to a wife, "I've stayed with you all these years because it was good for me"? Would it be that much better than saying, "I left you because it was fun for me"? The decision was still "for me."

So the issue Tion brought to the forefront was this: Would I live "for me" or for others and God? Because of the depression I was feeling, the impulse to run away from my life and drown my mind in some form of escape was almost overpowering. But I can see now that God let me drain the last drop of my own resources so that I might slake my thirst at His own well.

Unprovoked, Downward-Reaching, Creative Love

It seems strange that someone who was a long-time Christian, in a stable marriage, who had friends, children, and a good dog, would have any deficiency in the love department. But I did.

The reason for this was that I suffered from an incomplete *definition* of love, which led to an incomplete *experience*. " 'Out of the abundance of the heart the mouth speaks' " Jesus said (Matthew 12:34, NKJV), meaning that we act upon what is inside of us. Our internal environment expresses itself in our words and behaviors. If we are "programmed" to believe love is a certain way, we will love in just that way. And my way of loving was defective because my software had a glitch.

Part of the reason my conception of love was truncated was because of a linguistic limitation. The English language only had one word for all the varied types of love. This was a problem because "while words express thoughts, it is also true that thoughts follow words."[1] The more we express something in a limited way, the more we limit our concept of it.

Let me illustrate this. My firstborn used to call every small furry animal a "dog," because her tiny, uncoordinated tongue could say that word easily. As she grew, however, she learned "cat," "squirrel," and "skunk." Her knowledge of animals expanded along with her vocabulary, and now at fifteen years old, she is very well-rounded in her knowledge of animal species.

In the same way, we might increase our vocabulary in the love department and experience concurrently an increase in our knowledge of it. But our language doesn't accommodate this—we use one word for love that is Holy and the same word for love that is wholly Hollywood.

As I studied the idea of love from a gospel perspective, I discovered that the languages of the Bible each had several words for love. Greek, in particular, had four: *storge,* or motherly, familial love: *phileo,* or brotherly love; *eros,* or sexual love; and last but not least, *agape,* the New Testament word for divine love.

Now that my language could isolate God's kind of love from human love, I could sharpen my focus on exactly what constituted God's love. How was it different? What made it unique? Although the 1888 messengers didn't use the Greek words for love, Waggoner really nailed one primary distinction between God's love and human love.

Sometimes when a declaration of love is made, the loved one asks, "Why do you love me?" Just as if anybody could give a reason for love! Love is its own reason. If the lover can tell just why he loves another, that very answer shows that he does not really love. . . . Love loves, simply because it is love. Love is the quality of the individual who loves, and he loves because he has love, irrespective of the character of the object.[2]

Waggoner had obtained his idea of love straight from the Bible, which tells us that, "[love] is *not provoked"* (1 Corinthians 13:5, emphasis mine). Typically, we envision someone choking back a temper tantrum when we hear this, and the word can apply in that sense. But there is another way of looking at provocation. If I can be provoked to irritation or impatience, can't I be provoked to affection as well? Isn't the essence of love that it is not altered by human behavior? One meaning of "provoked" is "to stimulate." Love is not *stimulated* to either negative or positive emotion. It isn't stirred up or modified by something in the one being loved, it is just there regardless, whether it is *provoked* or not.

This is not to say that love is emotionless. On the contrary, love that does not rely on provocation can be intensely passionate because it is rooted in God, the One who masterminded our capacity for affection. Within the boundaries of principle, emotions have opportunity to deepen and enrich that they do not have if they are dependent upon fickle love-triggers and flights of feeling.

This principle-based concept of love revealed to me that God's love was constant toward me. It also meant that if I received God's love into my heart, my love for my husband, my children, and even my worst enemies would be constant and unchanging. Even now I think about this, and I am struck dumb.

Another characteristic of *agape* is that it is downward reaching. The action of *agape* does not reach up to enrich self, but it reaches down to enrich another, for Jesus "poured out His soul unto death" (Isaiah 53:12, NKJV). During this discovery period of my life, I read anew the passage that is now my favorite in all the Bible, Philippians 2:5-8 (see below). It told me that Jesus had made such a downward journey, from the highest heaven to the lowest hell, in order to save humanity.

All that the world teaches us about love—and much of what religion teaches us—leads us to think love reaches up to something higher in order to acquire something. "We are climbing Jacob's ladder," we sing, but are we climbing *up* Jacob's ladder, or was Jacob's ladder rather a metaphor of Jesus climbing *down* to us so that He could carry us back up? True love is based upon self-giving rather than self-getting, I realized. Waggoner, the little whippersnapper, had this down as well:

> The highest human conception of love is to love because we are loved, or because the object of our love is lovable. But God loves the unlovely. He loves those who hate Him.[3]

We find it so hard to grasp this characteristic because from both within and without we hear messages to the contrary. From within, our self-exalting natures tell us that we need to seek to "love" people who can do something for us. From without, our culture is more and more given over to self-enrichment, which leads people to regard self-surrender as a liability. Studies show that "fewer than half of all adult Americans today regard the idea of sacrifice for others as a positive moral virtue."[4] It's the wimp that give up himself for others, we are told. This attitude results in a dearth of truly love-based relationships.

> The reason there are so many hardhearted men and women in the world is that true affection has been regarded as weakness, and has been discouraged and repressed.[5]

When the essence is bilked out of love in this way, the greatest sufferers are children, the elderly, and the poor. These people have little to give except themselves and are often trampled by a society that is constantly grasping to acquire. True love, by contrast, will throw dinner parties for people who will never invite us back (see Luke 14:13). It will seek opportunities to build up those who are weak (see 1 Corinthians 12:23), and yes, it will love those who hate us (see Matthew 5:44).

A third characteristic of divine love is that it is creative. While love does not depend upon the value of the object, it does *create* value. Christ died for us when we were "without strength," "sinners," and "enemies," (Romans 5: 6, 8 and 10, NKJV) but we are assured that God "will make a mortal more rare than fine gold, a man more than the golden wedge of Ophir" (Isaiah 13:12, NKJV). We may have no intrinsic value, but God's love *causes* us to become valuable. When we can believe this, we will rise to the occasion and become all God has designed we should be.

This was the case with Mary Magdalene. While she was a complete waste when Jesus found her, "Christ saw in Mary capabilities for good."

He also knew "the circumstances that had shaped her life. He might have extinguished every spark of hope in her soul, but He did not."[6] He comes to us today and every day, assuring us that He, as Creator, can create in us the value that we have lost because of sin.

Let me illustrate this creative power. As I struggled to use what was left of my voice, there was one individual who helped me immensely. Dave was a fantastic singer himself, someone who could have easily made me cower with feelings of inferiority. He opened his mouth, and out came a silvery stream of music. Often he was accompanied by his wife's exceptionally rich soprano voice. Dave had more than a musical gift, though—he had a heart that was very compassionate toward hurting people. I can remember going to him before a performance, ready to cancel. Dave took me over the scales, all the while encouraging me and showing me how to use what was left.

Then there were the pep talks, "You having voice problems again? Well, I listen to you sing, and I think it sounds good! It may not be what you had, but use what you have left! I'll take 70% of Jen any day! You can do it, girl!" The fact that he thought I could still sing did more than amaze me—it inspired me. Resting on his knowledge of the voice and confidence that I could still make music, I re-learned the art of vocalizing. His belief in me as a singer was contagious! Dave is to some degree responsible for the fact that I continued to sing beyond that crisis point.

Many listless souls wander this planet, never reaching their potential because they don't sense that anyone believes in them. Sometimes all it takes is one encouraging comment and a spark of hope lights the way for years to come. If we saw the power of encouragement for what it is, we would more often speak a " 'word in season to him who is weary' " (Isaiah 50:4, NKJV).

God Himself believes in us. One searching question asked in God's word is, "What if some did not believe? Will their unbelief make the faithfulness of God without effect?" (Romans 3:3, NKJV). Since a better translation of "faithfulness" in this verse is "faith," the verse is asking if God's *faith* will eventually see fruit, and the answer, of course, is yes. Our unbelief does not ruin God's faith that humanity will at long last respond to Him with complete self-surrender, becoming vessels of His faithful love to everyone we know. There is power in this idea! If one person's faith in another can give steam to drive them to great attainments, how much more will God's faith push us beyond our limits.

Hand in Hand With the True Gospel

The characteristics of *agape* are unique and need constant reinforcement. We are told to "Behold *what manner* of love the Father has bestowed upon us" (1 John 3:1, NKJV, emphasis mine). The *manner* or *kind* of love is in contrast to what we normally accept as love. Once we begin to see it, we will begin to be it, so to speak, and we will manifest a motivating principle that is in sharp contrast to the principles of the world. True love is an aggravating rebuke to those who don't have it, and their reaction will be animosity, for "all who desire to live godly in Christ Jesus will suffer persecution" (2 Timothy 3:12, NKJV). Because true, godly love always brings persecution, we can assume when we *aren't* persecuted that we probably don't have the real thing.

I know there is Christian persecution in faraway places, but there is really very little in the Western world. This stems from the fact that Christianity's idea of love has been polluted since the days of the early church. *Agape* has been mingled with self-centered love in Christian thinking until its power to transform has been neutralized. It is with a restoration of the true gospel that the characteristics of divine love will again become clear. While there is any legalism at all in our understanding of salvation, the focus will always be upon man climbing up to reach God. It is when we understand the gospel that our focus shifts to God coming down to reach man and give him the free gift of righteousness. This is why the idea of *agape* love and the message of righteousness by faith are like hand in glove.

Once I realized that Jesus' love was not provoked, that there was nothing I could do to make it come or go away, that it was downward-reaching rather than upward-grasping, and that He was busy creating me anew in His image, I was ready to learn to love others in the same way He loved me. There they were before me; two tiny, helpless children who needed to be taught how to live, a husband who worked too hard because he had to, a circle of friends and acquaintances that were just as messed up as I was.

Yes, I was devastated, yes I longed for escape, but as the enemy of love presented his options, I scratched them off one by one. I couldn't live like Tion, leaving pain behind as I ran from my own. No, beholding the manner of love the Father had bestowed upon me in Jesus Christ implanted that same love within me. I would receive that love, then I would, in my faltering way, love those He put in my path. In the light of His great sacrifice, how could I choose otherwise?

Speaking of that great sacrifice, it was the study of the cross of Calvary that expanded my conception of love even further. I still have a long way to go, but I would like to share more of my journey thus far. The next two chapters will take a closer look at *agape* in the light of the Cross.

> *Let this mind be in you which was also in Christ Jesus, who, being in the form of God, did not consider it robbery to be equal with God, but made Himself of no reputation, taking the form of a bondservant, and coming in the likeness of men. And being found in appearance as a man, He humbled Himself and became obedient to the point of death, even the death of the cross (Philippians 2:5-8, NKJV).*

---

1. Ellen White, *The Ministry of Healing,* page 251.

2. E. J. Waggoner, *The Glad Tidings,* page 116.

3. Ibid.

4. Barbara Dafoe Whitehead, "Dan Quayle Was Right," *The Atlantic Monthly,* April, 1993, page 7.

5. Ellen White, *The Desire of Ages,* page 516.

6. Ibid., page 568.

CHAPTER EIGHT

Agape, the Intruding Force

My children were toddlers, not old enough to help pack for a trip but old enough to think they could. We were headed to Florida for Christmas, and Mommy and kids would go first; Daddy would come later. That meant Mommy was the "alpha and omega" of the packing and traveling ritual.

I had to hover closely enough over the little ducklings to make sure they didn't pack a suitcase full of swimsuits and nothing else, but remain distant enough to avoid insulting them with the insinuation that they couldn't manage alone. It was an exhausting day, but finally their suitcases, all six of them (I have two children), were packed and waiting by the door, and they themselves were tucked neatly in bed, totally unconscious.

Now I could stumble through my own packing with my eyes at half-mast, hoping my semi-comatose state didn't cause me to forget something crucial, like clothes. Then there were business details to tie up, pets to house, airport convenes to coordinate and Christmas presents to wrap. Finally, at midnight I set my alarm for 4 A.M. and flopped into bed muttering, "I will sleep on the plane tomorrow."

On the plane tomorrow, which in four wee hours became today, I was reminded of the foremost rule of airplane seating etiquette; the middle seat is for mommies. In other words, no one wants the middle seat, and in the pecking order of preferences, Mommy's preferences come last. So there I was, the one who vowed she would sleep, sitting between two toddlers on their way to see Gramma and a bunch of Christmas presents with their names on it. They carried with them an atmosphere that was about as conducive to sleep as a playpen full of Mexican jumping beans. I tried tipping my seat back and laying my head on the headrest, but one of them accidentally smacked me in the nose. I put my elbow on the armrest and rested my tired head in my hand, but one of them knocked my arm out from under me.

My exhaustion overcame me. I envisioned almost simultaneously my hands wrapped tightly around a little neck and headlines in Tampa Bay's morning paper declaring the same. No, murder is not the answer, I thought—reading is. I pulled out the book I happened to be reading, which was E. J. Waggoner's *Waggoner on Romans*, and opened it to the bookmark. My eyes literally fell on the following passage. I could almost hear Waggoner speaking plaintively:

"What is patience? It is endurance of suffering. . . ."

Oh, I don't believe it, I thought. He nailed me! I read on:

> "The root of the word 'patience' means suffering. We see this in the fact that one who is ill is called "a patient" that is, he is a sufferer. People often excuse their petulance by saying that they have so much to endure. They think that they would be patient if they did not have to suffer so much. No, they would not be. There can be no patience where there is no suffering. Trouble does not destroy patience, but develops it. When trouble seems to destroy one's patience, it is simply showing the fact that the person had no patience."[1]

I realized at that moment what God was trying to say. I had no patience, but this patience-testing circumstance was the perfect opportunity for me to get it. I couldn't even *achieve* patience without something to test it! In short, patience, like all the attributes of love, requires suffering.

I felt my nerves decompress and the muscles of my neck release. The rest of the flight was no different as far as the external circumstances were concerned. The Mexican jumping beans continued doing the cha-cha, which caused several more accidental blows and continued intrusion upon my personal space. I was still exhausted and still unable to sleep, but I was different inside. I was drinking from a deeper well that fortified me for life's irritations by showing me how God could use them. Finally I could say, "I will rather boast in my infirmities, that the power of Christ may rest upon me" (2 Corinthians 12:9, NKJV).

This experience in child rearing, and so many others, has provided a window into the fourth characteristic of *agape*—self-sacrifice.

Suffering Love

Suffering is innate to love. Why? Because the fallen creation is calibrated to work in opposition to love, so love requires going against nature. Nature includes our human nature, also calibrated in the school of self-centeredness, which opposes the existence of love within us. *Agape* love is an intruding force in this world, causing an alarm reaction befitting an alien invasion whenever it is manifest. There is no chance for negotiating peace between the two worlds, either. Something must die— *agape* or nature. It is God's will that nature dies and *agape* lives.

This is called self-denial, a foreign concept to this world where "me-ism" increasingly reigns. It is different than self-discipline in that self-discipline practices *temporary* denial in order to secure lasting fulfillment. Self-discipline delays gratification in order to have greater gratification in the end. There is nothing innately Christian about self-discipline, and it shouldn't be confused with Christianity because any strong-willed egotist can practice self-discipline without one drop of the Holy Spirit's infusion.

Self-denial, on the other hand, takes the working of a power outside of ourselves. It is not temporary nor does it seek greater gratification. It is a complete surrender of self, forever. Embodied in it is this: that the Father denied Himself (gave) His Son, and that Son denied Himself His Father, that we might be saved.

Can you look at that reality and not be gashed open in remorse? If you can, you need to take a closer look, something we can all afford to do at any time, something the Lord tried to lead His church to do in 1888, and something we will do right now.

Seeing is Being

A staid focus on the closing scenes of Christ's life will characterize the Christians of the last days of earth's history. It is from this well that

God's followers will draw their motivation to remain loyal to Him through the greatest test that has ever come upon humankind—the test of the mark of the beast. Biblical accounts of the last days depict a time when faithfulness to God will necessitate passing through a trial so severe that only fully mature Christians will maintain their fidelity.

What characterizes the people who pass this test? The fact that they "follow the Lamb wherever He goes" (Revelation 14:4). "The Lamb" refers to Christ in His office of self-giving Redeemer. The remnant people do not, in this scenario, "follow the *Lion* wherever He goes," or even "follow the *Creator*" or "follow the *Law-Giver,*" although obviously, they are one and the same divine Person, Jesus Christ. This reference to the self-giving of Christ shows that God's last-day people will follow the spirit of self-denial manifest by the Lamb as He hung upon the cross of Calvary. In short, God's followers will be selfless.

The Power of Identity

How can self-entrenched human beings ever come to this point? By a simple dynamic called beholding. It works in two steps:

1. I come to identify with what I spend time observing.
2. I become like what I identify with.

Why did I iron my wavy hair as a teenager? Because I came to identify with the models in the fashion magazines, whom I spent time observing (They all had stick-straight hair!). Eventually, I conformed myself to what I identified with, even if it meant risking burning my hair off. The same thing can work in the positive. I can learn to identify with Christ and in so doing be conformed to His image.

But what is the initial attraction to Him? Something must grab our attention to lead us to even *want* to spend time beholding Him. As mentioned previously, the foundation of "What did Jesus do?" must be in place before I can be properly motivated to do anything good, including spending time with God. So many of our attempts at devotion are ritualistic and dry. Shouldn't it be our *desire* to seek the Lord? If so, what will spark that desire? What will make us *want* to start identifying with Him?

For me, it has been discovering how closely He first identified with me. This was a prominent feature of the 1888 message and played a huge role in enticing me into a deeper study life. I saw that Jesus became "like His brethren," identifying Himself so completely with sinners that He identified with sin itself and suffered the wrath of God as if

He Himself was a sinner. This drew me into fellowship with Him. How? Let me give you an illustration from my own life. It's not pretty, but it will get the point across.

One of the most isolating experiences I can draw up out of my childhood memory bank was being molested by a group of kids on the playground at school. Yes, molested, as in physically, sexually, and everyally molested. You don't need to hear the details, but I remember it so vividly that I can relive it as if it happened yesterday. I can still see the faces flashing back and forth between mean and angry to mocking laughter as this group of kids literally sabotaged me emotionally and physically. There was absolutely nothing I could do about it, and I had no way to defend myself. As a result, I know what it is to be violated and helpless to stop it.

This event was no more than an embarrassing memory until I saw it in the light of Christ's humanity. Jesus, in becoming man, subjected Himself to all the trials and temptations that afflict men and women, including the trauma of abuse, and in so doing walked into my private hell in order to reach me. That Jesus would subject Himself to torture and mockery, that He would embrace as part of the Father's plan the Cross and all the abuse that it involved, touched my heart in a way nothing else could. Consider these statements pertaining to Calvary:

> "At the hands of the beings whom He had created, and for whom He was making an infinite sacrifice, He received every indignity."[3]

> "Never was criminal treated in so inhuman a manner as was the Son of God."[4]

The point of this is not to try to prove that Jesus was sexually molested, but it *is* to prove that His dignity was violated, horribly. Essentially, all abuse is the same in this respect. The difference between His abuse and mine, however, is that in His case it was avoidable. He could have called ten thousand angels, or just pointed one Sovereign finger at the idiots and reduced them to an ash heap. Why didn't He? Because He relished the opportunity to come near to me where I am. Not many people have come to the part of me that was isolated that day on the playground, but Jesus has. He came through the obstacle course of my pain so that He could look me in the eye and say, "I know how you feel."

And do you know what? I believe Him. I read the account of the Cross, and the nearness of Christ becomes perceptibly real. I see in Him a high and holy God who came down to the level of humanity on every point except participation in sin itself. I see the ugly faces surrounding Him and sense His yearning for sympathy. I feel the invasion of hateful hands that crawled over His body in swarms and the gashing of implements of torture. I taste the blood and smell the spit dripping down His kind face. I see Him in the midst of all this, looking straight into my soul and saying, "I am here to find *you*. I am earning the right to your affections and your worship. I am touched, forever touched, with the feeling of your weakness."

Somehow, my spirit's frontier is transformed. The wilderness is tamed, and a clear path that leads to the throne of God is in clear view. I want nothing more than to follow this Jesus who followed me first into the wilds of sin and sadness. I want to rest in His presence, to know all there is to know about Him.

Once I am drawn into fellowship with Jesus, the law of beholding begins to unfold itself in my life.

1. I come to identify with Jesus as I spend time observing Him.
2. I become like Jesus as I identify with Him.

It is simple but very, very potent. This identifying with Christ will produce the same spirit of self-denial in His followers that He Himself exemplified. Once I have been touched with His identification with me, I not only identify with Him, but I feel naturally compelled to identify with fellow sinners. In this way, the love of Christ awakens love, not just love for Him, but love among people.

It is not the mighty, the disciplined, the gritty, or the gifted that will finally and fully reflect Him to the world; it is the weakest of the weak, the helpless, the hurting like you and me. The opportunity to come into the closest fellowship with Him is open to any and all that are willing to follow the Lamb. This will naturally produce Christian character and, with it, the spirit of self-giving.

Giving to Get

But much of our religion today indicates more self-discipline than self-denial. We may "give up" certain things, but we see them as a means to gain something greater. We sing of "joy by and by," seeing the trials of life as a kind of price we pay for a waiting reward. The only difference between those of us who view the keeping of God's law as an act of penance that will gain heaven, and the Catholic monk of the Dark Ages wearing a hair shirt, is that the monk does what is not required while we take what is required and transform it into an act of self-salvation. Waggoner said this was like "crucifying ourselves on our own crosses. . . . We were antichrist ourselves, and all the time we were doing that, we were throwing stones at the pope."[5]

Although God works with us where we are, self-centered motivations are limited in what they can produce. If we rest satisfied in them, we are bound to regress into this kind of salvation by works. While I have no burden to belittle the reality of our heavenly home, it is a sad thing when our motivations go no deeper than longing for streets of gold and an end to taxes. Wouldn't it bring comfort to Christ's heart to know that we were serving Him, not to gain heaven or lose hell, but because we love Him?

When the world is divided into two camps, every character will be fully developed. This means that the motivations of the heart will come to fruition, and there will be no hiding who we really are. We have the privilege today of allowing God to transform and purify our motives to the point where we are clear channels through which He can shine. No, we aren't there yet, and anyone who claims to be is giving conclusive proof that he's not. We are, however, called to operate on better motives than fear of punishment and hope of reward. A realization of Christ's identity with me and my subsequent identification with Him will produce those better motives.

Ah, but I haven't even scratched the surface of this phenomenon called self-sacrifice. We see glimmers of it in the Crucifixion, but we see it in its zenith at the Cross.

You see, the Cross was much more than the Crucifixion. What really happened at Calvary was as far beyond mere human abuse and physical torture as cancer is beyond a flea bite. Yet the physical and emotional sufferings of Christ at the hands of men do help us understand the soul-agony He suffered at the hands of God by giving us a reference point from which to work. As we hear of the blood and bruises, the interrogation and abuses, the degree of empathy we feel serves as a launching pad for our journey into the realms of the soul suffering, which we naturally have a dimmer conception of. The next step in my journey, hopefully a journey you will continue to share with me, was to take a hard look at what it was about Calvary that constituted the greatest sacrifice ever made.

Emmanuel, God with us
Oh, what a sacred thought!
A holy God born human
In form of those He sought
A Sunbeam in the shadows
A Rose amid the thorns
A King among the common He was born

Emmanuel, God with us
And even more than this
The Sun was wrapped in darkness
The Rose in ugliness
The King laid down His scepter
His crown He put aside
And looked like any man who lived and died

Emmanuel, God with us
My heart is strangely warmed
And in my foggy thinking
A pure conception formed
Identifying with me
He turned away from sin
And now I can identify with Him

Emmanuel, God with us
A holy God involved
In sin's pathetic problem
And finally, it's solved
A Blossom in the refuse
A Lily in the dirt
Sweet Flower, for our sakes forever hurt

Emmanuel, God with us
Today still coming near

The bleeding of His brothers
On battle grounds of fear
Five wounds to prove His oneness
Five wounds are proof enough
We see Him in our flesh and call Him Love.

_____

1. E. J. Waggoner, *Waggoner on Romans,* page 5.94.
2. Ellen White, *Steps to Christ,* page 58.
3. Ellen White, *The Desire of Ages,* page 700.
4. Ibid., page 710.
5. E. J. Waggoner, *Christ and His Righteousness,* page 190.

CHAPTER NINE

The Soul of Sacrifice

More than any other subject, the cross of Christ has gripped me. Although as far back in my life as my conversion to Christ I sensed its power, there was a period when it came into clearer focus than it had theretofore. During this period, the Spirit seemed to be urging me through various channels to delve deeper and deeper into this mystery.

Once when some friends and I were on a concert tour, our car broke down. While we waited for repairs, we stayed in the mechanic's home, and his wife handed me a book entitled *Even the Death of the Cross.* It was a humble, staple-spined study published by an independent ministry that I had always heard was very fanatical. My prejudices were overcome by boredom, though, and I read the entire book in a day or two. A short time later, I read a book entitled *In Search of the Cross,* which also led me to my knees. My heart was warmed as I recognized that God was leading various ones within His body to take a closer look at the focal point of the gospel story.

As I began a more serious look at the Cross, I realized that it was the driving force behind the message of 1888. Even though the writings of Jones and Waggoner don't have much systematic study on the subject, the elements of the Cross are present and woven throughout their messages. Because my awakening to the gospel and the Cross were so simultaneous, I can't talk about one without including the other. Surely, "The sacrifice of Christ as an atonement for sin is the great truth around which all other truths cluster."[1]

I hope you don't think me presumptuous if I tell you that I have found a cure for the love of sin. Whenever the world has a grip on me, be it through temptation, discouragement, anger, or apathy, there is one thing that never fails to break through the walls of my heart and bring me back to God. I walk with Jesus from Gethsemane to Calvary, through the six trials, the five scenes of abuse, the four condemnations, the two scourgings and the Crucifixion. My feminine heart is overwhelmed with sympathy for His humiliation, and my humanity shrinks from His pain, but something much more happens. As I strain to comprehend what it means that He "became a curse for us," I see that His love outstretches anything I have ever known. Almost imperceptibly, my heart turns from myself to Him, and I come to desire more than anything to see happiness mark the face that was "marred more than any man" (Isaiah 52:14). Quietly but effectively the power of sin is broken by the revelation of His love.

The Crucifixion

The Gospels give no elaborate description of the Crucifixion, probably because it was so common that the writers considered the details to be superfluous. Since we have no such familiarity, in order to see the Cross for what it is, we need to see the Crucifixion for what it was. But there is another impedance besides our ignorance; the reality of crucifixion has been evicted by an *unreal* depiction of it. Many masterpiece paintings portray, for instance, an uninjured body with a loin covering carefully draped from the cross and an angelic sweetness in the facial expression of our Lord. Nothing could be further from the truth. Even in the most graphic passion play the horror of the ordeal is muted to our senses. Our ignorance of the reality of crucifixion does not displace these false renderings, though, and so we accept them as true. Let's remove the fuzzy lens from our camera and look at a few of the stark, cruel facts.

Jesus was arrested Thursday night, deprived of sleep, food, and water and marched through the next hellish half-day as He was harassed, humiliated, and beaten. During the following trials and scenes of abuse, He was interrogated by numerous enemies and five times battered and abused by haughty priests, civic authorities, and sub-humans alike. By the time His last trial before Pilate arrived, Christ was already "covered with wounds."[2]

More than this, the sensitive emotions of the God-Man were violated beyond imagination. "To be surrounded by human beings under the control of Satan was revolting to Him."[3] This sensitivity factor alone was enough to make the cross of Christ a more excruciating ordeal than the cross of a common criminal.

The scourging that Pilate used to attempt to circumvent the crucifixion utilized a short whip consisting of several heavy leather thongs with small balls of lead attached near the ends. The thongs would cut while the balls would bruise, until the back of the condemned was "hanging in long ribbons and the entire area was an unrecognizable mass of torn, bleeding tissue."[4] The two scourgings alone brought Jesus to the brink of death.

There is archeological evidence that Jesus was crucified on a "T" shaped cross, rather than the Latin cross we typically see in paintings. Although the vertical beam was fixed in the ground, the horizontal beam, called the patibulum, was carried by the criminal to the execution site, and weighed about 110 pounds. Because of extensive exhaustion and blood loss, Jesus was unable to bear this weight although He courageously tried. By this time shock may very well have set in.

Jesus was probably nailed to the cross through the wrists because the nails through the hands would strip through the fingers and fail to support the weight of the body. The same thick, square nails were driven through the metatarsal bones of His feet. Once upon the cross, Jesus had to push up from His feet to breathe successfully, and so He alternated between shock waves of pain through His arms, near suffocation, and searing pain through His legs and feet.

The Cross

But deep within the Being of Infinite Love there rolled a storm cloud of suffering that made all other stresses pale in comparison. So profound was this pain that it swallowed up all others the way labor makes a woman forget everything around her. The very worst was happening—the one thing that He couldn't live without was fading away. The love of His Father was eluding His awareness and the frown of Heaven's condemnation was taking its place. This looming fear so pressed upon our Messiah that "His physical pain was hardly felt."[5]

What? He could *hardly feel* deep lacerations that shredded His flesh, pulsing, green-gray bruises and nails through His wrists? He was nearly oblivious to the horror of suffocation and the dizzying effect of blood loss and dehydration? Could fear of losing God's smile really distract from such duress? Yes, yes, and yes.

Consider this. Even considering the physical trauma He endured before the Crucifixion, Jesus was not expected to die as quickly as He did. Because the Jewish leaders did not want to leave the crucified bodies hanging on the cross lest the Sabbath be desecrated, they sanctimoniously proposed that the Lord of the Sabbath be taken off His cross, along with the two thieves. In order to hasten death, they broke the legs of the thieves, but Jesus was found to be already dead within six hours of crucifixion. At the request of the priests, a Roman soldier pierced His side, and "there flowed two copious and distinct streams, one of blood and the other of water." We are assured that this proved that Jesus "died of a broken heart."[6]

"My heart is like wax," the prophet spoke, "it is melted within me" (Psalm 22:14). The medical term for this "broken heart" is *pericardial effusion.* It simply refers to the sack surrounding the heart filling with fluid and creating a crushing inward pressure. This condition is brought on by extreme stress, and in the case of Jesus it was physical, emotional, mental, and spiritual.

What was this anguish that literally poisoned the life streams of the Son of God so that He could hardly notice the physical torture He was undergoing? This question has loomed large in my mind and awed me over and over. The best I can do in trying to comprehend what Jesus endured for me is to sink into the inspired accounts and pray . . . *pray* that God gives me understanding.

Jesus "humbled Himself and became obedient to the point of death, *even the death of the cross"* (Philippians 2:8, NKJV, emphasis mine). This death embraces more than the millions of martyrdoms that have been suffered by God's followers throughout the ages, and it involves more than mere crucifixion itself. There was something unique and unprecedented about the death of Christ, who started out "in the form of God," which is the highest place in the entire universe, and ended up on a cross. If He began in the highest heaven, wouldn't it be consistent with the downward-reaching motion of divine love if He who began there would exhaust the limits of *agape* and find Himself in the lowest hell? Yes, as nearly sacrilegious as it sounds, Jesus went to *hell* to save us.

Hell, or the "the lake of fire," is the place where the final annihilation of the wicked will take place. Hell is the end of existence and the beginning of extinction for whoever finds themselves there. This is hard for us to grasp in that we have no reference point for it. The deaths we encounter are merely a temporary unconsciousness from which all will one day rise again when " 'there will be a resurrection of the dead, both the just and the unjust' " (Acts 24:15, NKJV).

This death that takes place " 'in hell' " is of " 'both soul and body' " (Matthew 10:28). The eternal consequence is what makes this "second death" unique, and what made the death of Christ as great a sacrifice as it was. No one save Jesus Himself has experienced the second death.

Because the Cross symbolized this utter extinction, the Jewish leaders wished to see Jesus hung on it. Recall that at least twice they attempted to stone Jesus (see John 8:59 and 10:31) and once to throw Him over a cliff (see Luke 4:29, 30). By the end of His ministry, however, these hypocrites were so filled with malice toward Him that only crucifixion would do. They might have executed Him in one of these other ways without insuring the complicity of Rome, but for crucifixion they must convince Roman authorities that He was deserving of it. This was a difficult task in that this method of execution was reserved for runaway slaves and other serious offenders, not political/religious figures whose worst crime was stirring up the multitudes. Still, the Jewish leaders were willing to struggle against the odds because only a cross would do for this Jesus called Christ.

Recalling the directive given by Moses that if an executed criminal was hung on a tree he was "cursed of God," these religionists determined to make this commentary concerning Christ. (See Deuteronomy 21:23.) *Cursed,* again, meant eternal destruction. Most death-sentenced criminals could still receive forgiveness from God. But if the judge determined that the one having received the sentence of death was beyond even God's forgiveness, he would order him to be hung on a tree that a solemn warning might be given of the gravity of placing oneself beyond the reach of divine help.

Notice how intent the Jewish leaders were to have this said about Christ. Pilate attempted a total of twelve times to dissuade them and ensure His release. "I find no fault in Him at all!" he cried into their intractable ears. He sent Him to Herod, but Herod sent Him back. After the report came of his wife's terrifying dream, Pilate tried to have Him set free under the Roman custom that allowed for the release of one prisoner. They chose Barabbas. Then Pilate hoped scourging Him would satisfy their bloodlust. No, the spurting blood from the veins deep in the back of the Sin Bearer only made them thirst for more. "Shall I crucify your king?" Pilate asked in disbelief. "We have no king but Caesar!" they cried, sealing their fate as a people. Their passionate hate for Christ overcame even their passionate love for the Jewish nation. Pilate trembled in fear of a Jewish uprising and finally capitulated to their plan. The cooperation of Rome was secured, and Christ was Golgotha-bound.

The Jewish nation condemned Him. Amazingly, Rome yielded to their plan. More amazing still is the fact that heaven yielded to it all! Not one mighty angel, no thundering voice, no natural disaster or political interposition was ordained to keep Christ from His cross. This is because it was God's plan, not theirs. Actually, the powers that sought His destruction were doing the yielding without knowing it.

There is nothing meritorious about submitting to abuse. Even Jesus told His disciples to "flee" if they were persecuted (see Matthew 10:23), and His own avoidance of stoning showed that He was in no rush to die a martyr's death. But when the hour had come, He submitted Himself to the condemnation of unjust religious and civil authorities that He might come under the just condemnation of Heaven, " 'being delivered by the determined purpose and foreknowledge of God' " (Acts 2:23, NKJV), "that He, by the grace of God, might taste death for everyone," (Hebrews 2:9, NKJV). This He did with a firm resolve, which was arrived at in the Garden, and tested on the Cross.

The Glory of God in the Face of Jesus

"The glory of God," we are told in 2 Corinthians 4:6, is "in the face of Christ." Could this be literally true? Witness the *face* of Christ throughout these closing scenes. His changing countenance provides a window into His soul, and shows us what it was about His trial and crucifixion that brought Him soul-piercing sorrow and death.

One of the first signs of the agony of separation from God is seen by the stuporous disciples when Jesus wakes them after His first prayer in Gethsemane. "They hardly knew Him, His face was so changed by anguish."[7] During the second prayer, Jesus begins to sweat blood and again the disciples "saw His face marked with the bloody sweat of agony, and they were filled with fear."[8] When He prays the third and final time, however, Jesus reaches the conclusion that He will save man at any cost to Himself, and the sense of dread abated for a time. Judas appeared with the mob, and "no traces of His recent agony were visible as Jesus stepped forth to meet His betrayer."[9]

Pilate is amazed upon His first encounter with the Savior, for "on His face he saw no sign of guilt, no expression of fear, no boldness or defiance."[10] Finally, a scourged and exhausted Jesus appears before the people, side by side with the criminal Barabbas.

> Stripped to the waist, His back showed the long, cruel stripes, from which the blood flowed freely. His face was stained with blood, and bore the marks of exhaustion and pain; but never had it appeared more beautiful than now. The Savior's visage was *not marred* before His enemies.[11]

It wasn't until Christ again met the withdrawal of His Father's presence on the cross that the anguish within forced itself into expression. This time, however, the contortions of agony were so extreme that "God veiled the last human agony of His Son. . . . He was mercifully hidden by the mantle of God."[12]

Can you see it? The changing expressions of our Lord throughout His trial and crucifixion are like the changing patterns in clouds that reveal the building pressure and brewing storms in the atmosphere. Placidity marked Him during the worst abuse that humans could render, but at two times His face was twisted with overwhelming pain: the Garden and the Cross. It was there that He received the wound that even this Brave Soldier could not bear—the hiding of His Father's face.

Connecting to Him

We don't know what God-abandonment feels like, so how can we possibly relate to what our Forever Friend endured for us? Although nothing in our experience compares, God has allowed us small doses of His suffering that we might connect emotionally and spiritually to Him. There are several analogies the Bible uses to describe the Cross that are helpful in bringing us in touch with it. On the cross, Jesus was:

1. The Fatherless—"I was cast upon you from birth. From My mother's womb You have been My God" (Psalm 22:10, NKJV and Psalm 69:8, NKJV), Jesus said, but then, "I have become a stranger to my brothers, and an alien to my mother's children."

I asked my youngest child what she thought it must have been like for Jesus to die on the cross, and she replied, "It would be like if *you* tried to kill me, Mommy." For my child, the thought of being turned against by someone whom she had always trusted was the worst thing that could be. I think she expressed in those words the essence of what Jesus felt when the One with whom He had an intimate connection from eternity cast Him off. Jesus, ever the object of His Father's love, suddenly became an orphan.

Think of a time in your life when you have experienced abandonment by someone you were deeply connected to. Now multiply that by infinity and you have the Cross.

2. The Rejected—"He is despised and rejected of men, a Man of sorrows and acquainted with grief. And we hid, as it were, or faces from Him; He was despised, and we did not esteem Him" (Isaiah 53:3, NKJV).

My children have an expression for someone who is unpopular with their peers. "So and so," they say, "is *rejected."* Why do they choose that word from among so many to describe what it is to be singled out and spurned? Because rejection is the ultimate dread of a child during the years when they feel the need for acceptance most keenly. In this sense, Jesus became the rejected One in the school yard. Not only was Jesus cast off from His divine family, but He was ostracized by His friends and His people.

I recall being rejected by my peers in school. I could literally feel their hate-filled eyes burning holes in my back as I tried to ignore them. The sad thing was that I really longed for their acceptance and friendship. It is easy to be hated by people you hate, but being hated by those you love is a totally different story.

Think of a time when you have been ridiculed and scorned by your peers. Now imagine all your loved ones joining in with them, multiply that by infinity, and you have the Cross.

3. The condemned—"For He was cut off from the land of the living; for the transgressions of My people He was stricken. And they made His grave with the wicked" (Isaiah 53:8, 9, NKJV).

Guilt is a killer. Even for one innocently condemned, the sense of guilt provoked by the sentence of condemnation from a human court can be devastating. The amazing thing about the Cross was that Jesus felt our guilt as if it were His own. So real was the condemnation of His conscience that His self-worth crumbled. He must have cried like David, "I am a worm, and not a man, a reproach of men, and despised by the people" (Psalm 22:6).

Think of a time when you were found guilty of a crime. Imagine it being a crime punishable by death. Envision the hard faces of the official people as the execution takes place. Notice that no one cares, that they are glad to see you go. Multiply that by infinity, and you have the Cross.

His people abandoned Him. His nation condemned Him. And then seemingly, frighteningly, His God joined forces with the others. God has loved fatherless children, comforted rejected people, and forgiven condemned criminals since time began, but in Jesus' case, He couldn't do those things. God could not save humanity and at the same time save His Son from the effects of humanity's sin, and so He surrendered that dear Son to the cross, that He might become the God-forsaken God.

Strangely, I see in this God-abandoned Orphan the Father who will never leave me. I find acceptance in the tender arms that for me were nailed to a hard, cold symbol of rejection. From the Condemned I hear "neither do I condemn you," over and over again. *How can I ever thank You?* I ask, realizing that the greatest gift I can give Him is the glad acceptance of His gift. And I do accept it, Jesus, I do.

What will you do with this Jesus who said goodbye to life forever so that you could say "hello" to the same? Will you walk by this reality around which time itself revolves just for a few years of diversion? Will you let His precious blood soak into Judean soil without touching your life? Many years ago, A. T. Jones had similar questions:

> Will you let Him have you? Oh, does it call for too full a surrender? How full a surrender did He make? He surrendered all Himself; Christ gave up Himself, emptied Himself. The French translation is: He annihilated Himself —He undid Himself, and sank Himself in us, in order that God, instead of ourselves, and His righteousness, instead of our sinfulness, might be manifested in us instead of our sinful flesh. Then let us respond, and sink ourselves in Him, that God may still be manifest in sinful flesh[13]

Only One has ever died
Jesus Christ the crucified
High aloft an ugly tree
Where the damned alone should be
What is this? God's only Son
Anger's victim, nailed and hung
There to die with all our blame
Heaped upon His shattered frame

Not the pain of nail or spear
Nor the tauntings in His ear
Made His noble soul to quake
Made His holy heart to break
No, but human guilt compiled
Burdened Him, the undefiled
Purity our sin embraced
Then eternal death He faced

Wonder of the worlds of light
Mystery so infinite
Tell me of the Savior, tell
Of the love that went to hell

---

1. Ellen White, *Evangelism,* page 190.

2. Ellen White, *The Desire of Ages,* page 734.

3. Ibid., page 700.

4. Davis, Dr. C. Truman, *A Physician Testifies About the Crucifixion,* page 3 <www.konnections.com/Kcundick/crucifix.html>

5. Ellen White, *The Desire of Ages,* page 753.

6. Ibid., page 772.

7. Ibid., page 689.

8. Ibid., page 690.

9. Ibid., page 694.

10. Ibid., page 724.

11. Ibid., page 735.

12. Ibid., page 754.

13. Jones, A.T., *General Conference Bulletin,* 1895, page 303.

CHAPTER TEN

Promises, Promises

Dad had been in pain for a long time when finally a physician ordered an MRI. It was the worst possible news—cancer. And it was the worst possible cancer—pancreatic.

Pancreatic cancer. I hate those words.

Dad had an almost unsinkable faith in modern medicine. "We're gonna try to lick this thing," he said, "first with surgery, then with chemo, then radiation. . . . I know a fella who had pancreatic cancer. . . . He's doin' pretty good."

My consultations with physician friends weren't nearly so hopeful. Pancreatic cancer patients, if diagnosed early, may live five years if they are lucky, and Dad wasn't diagnosed early.

My sister and I drove eighteen hours straight to see him after his first operation. A funny quandary these surgeries present—you may remove the cancer, but then you may help the cancer remove you. Cancer cells are just clumps of over-oxidized molecules to begin with, so what do you do? You open up the body to the air and hope that the benefits will outweigh the risks. In Dad's case, they didn't.

Nine months later he informed us that he was dying. None of us believed him because he was still walking around, functioning, talking.

He called the family in from Connecticut, Massachusetts, Texas, and Kansas to come bid him farewell.

The Sabbath after we arrived, Dad gathered us all together in his bedroom, where he lay propped up in bed. He began what turned out to be three hours of us all making amends for wrongs done, reminiscing of good times, crying till our faces were red, and laughing till we cried again. After Dad had pronounced his "blessing" upon the family, he lay down, never to rise, eat, or talk again in this world.

Dad was an unbeliever, essentially. He had always attended church with Mom, but his answers to a few questions I asked when I was a teenager revealed his lack of religious faith. When I converted to Adventism, Dad just chalked it up to another one of my idiosyncrasies, but when my sister converted, Dad nearly had a nervous breakdown. She was his favorite child and Adventism his least favorite religion. As an act of protest to Kristin's conversion, Dad stopped attending church with my mom, fuming mad at the God he didn't believe in.

As he was dying, I was faced with the need to try to overcome the obstacles and talk to Dad about his salvation. There were hopeful signs. One quadriplegic friend, a Christian, had written to Dad, "I wish I could take this for you." Dad pulled Charlie's note out of a huge pile of get-well cards that came in stacks from all over the world (Dad was a much-loved man), read it and sobbed openly. I also observed a change in my Dad's attitude. He apologized for belittling my choices in life, including my religious ones, and he expressed more love in the months before his death than I had ever seen him express. Death can either harden or break a man, and Dad seemed to be breaking. Maybe, maybe, I would think, he is starting to open up to Christ.

My window of opportunity arrived only hours before Dad died. He couldn't talk or even see very well, but he heard our words as we tried to soothe his pain-wracked body. It was my shift at his bedside, so I played my guitar softly for him as a warm wind blew over us. The Spirit of God doesn't often tell me just what to do and when, but at this time He spoke, saying, "Now is the time."

"Dad," I whispered, "You have not been a religious man, but God still has a mansion prepared for you in heaven. You want to see us all again, Dad, I know you do. You can, Dad, please don't refuse to come. I know you can't talk, but even if you just say in your mind, 'Jesus, I accept You,' you can be saved. Just believe, Dad, right now, and we can all meet together in eternity. Follow along with me as I pray." Tears were pouring down his face as I prayed a simple sinner's prayer, and I know he heard every word.

Is my dad saved? I don't know what happened in his inmost heart, but I do know that God is big enough and generous enough and *God* enough to save a person on their deathbed. So I have hope.

And yes, I've thought about the thief on the cross, the prototype of all deathbed conversions. But there was a difference between him and my dad in that Dad couldn't even *talk.* This seemed to stretch the possibilities of salvation a little further than I even had a biblical precedent for. Still, I believe that if Dad believed, Jesus saved Him. When all a person has left are a few synaptic connections in the brain, when all electrical impulses to the body and mouth have failed, God can still honor the silent choice of someone who says "Yes" to Him, even if only in their thoughts.

The thing that amazed me about the whole deathbed scene with Dad was the sense I had that I had been prepared for that moment. If it had come at an earlier point in my Christian experience, I wouldn't have had the confidence that he was still savable, and I probably wouldn't have tried to lead him to Christ. Limiting God in who He can save leads us to a certain lack of assertiveness in our dealings with lost people. I think the reason I was able to hope against hope that Dad could be saved was because I understood the gospel.

Covenant of Grace, Covenant of Works

Sometimes we are uneasy with the idea of a person going all the way through life without serving God, then repenting upon their deathbed and being saved. Like the laborers in the parable, we see those who "worked" many fewer "hours" getting the same wages as us, who worked "all day" (see Matthew 20:1-16). The prodigal son's brother had a similar reaction (see Luke 15:11-32) when he faulted the father for celebrating the son's return. We, like them, naturally want some credit for our years of faithful service, but in this very attitude we manifest the fact that we have fallen from God's grace and are operating on the basis of works.

We have only two options in the matter of the means of salvation: works or grace. This issue has been reiterated over and over, but some things bear repeating.

The Bible contrasts works and grace in terms of the Old and New Covenants. Since a covenant is literally a promise, the Old Covenant is a promise of (human) works, and the New Covenant is a promise of (God's) grace. The Old Covenant was essentially man's promise to God, and the New is God's promise to man. Looking carefully at the history of the covenant God made with Abraham will show us the nature of these two options, at the same time making it plain that the only option that produces true obedience is grace.

God promised Abraham a son from whom would come a myriad of descendants. Abraham "believed in the Lord, and He accounted it to him for righteousness" (Genesis 15:6, NKJV). He hadn't done anything except believe, yet he was counted righteous! It is clear by looking at Abraham's performance over the next few years that he faltered and fell, but finally, at long last, he demonstrated obedience in the offering of Isaac.

As is manifest in the story of Abraham, the terms of God's covenant of grace are "believe and live." This belief will result in obedience because faith works (see Galatians 5:6), but because our faith is imperfect, it may take time, trial, and error, and we may each have an Ishmael or two before faith matures.

In the meantime, God "calls those things which do not exist as though they did" (Romans 4:17, NKJV), knowing that in the acorn of faith lies the oak of perfect obedience. God is willing to allow for a margin of error in our behavior as our faith grows, because He wants our obedience to be heartfelt. To suppress any foibles in our behavior, threatening to revoke our salvation as soon as our performance faltered would be to force us into a mode of fear, and our obedience would be merely external and robotic. Rather, God tolerates passing imperfection, that true heart-perfection may at last be seen.

This is not to say that there is anything fictitious about God's promise to make us obedient by grace. All the basic elements of perfect obedience are present in the exercise of true faith. It is actually *His* faith, the faith through which He rendered perfect obedience in human flesh, implanted within us. On the basis of what He accomplished while walking in our shoes, He can rest assured that we will, in partaking of His grace, accomplish the same.

The amazing thing about God's covenant of grace is that human beings would naturally rather have a works religion. Israel demonstrated this as God tried to reiterate Abraham's grace covenant at Sinai. They said, " 'All that the Lord has spoken we will do!' " (Exodus 19:8). What had He told them to do? Basically, believe a bunch of beautiful promises:

> " You have seen what I did to the Egyptians, and how I bore you on eagles' wings and brought you to Myself. Now therefore, if you will indeed obey My voice and keep My covenant, then you shall be a special treasure to Me above all people; for all the earth is Mine. And you shall be to Me a kingdom of priests and a holy nation" (vs. 4-6, NKJV).

A quick Hebrew lesson will illuminate this passage. "Obey" is from the Hebrew *shama*, which means, literally, "to hear": and "keep" is from the related *shamar,* which means, "to guard." "Covenant" is from the Hebrew *beriyth* and refers to "an obligation between a monarch and his subjects."[1] The passage could be paraphrased like this:

> If you will listen to My voice and guard My promise, My obligation to you, then you will be My unique people, powerful and holy.

God gave His children a list of things that He wanted to do for them and asked them to receive what He was giving them, but they responded with a legalistic promise to "do" what God had spoken. This was the Old Covenant, or the covenant of works, and man, not God, inaugurated it. God allowed the experiment to unfold because He knew that, if nothing else, Israel would learn the complete futility of self-trust.

Why would man choose a works program instead of salvation by grace? Chiefly because a works program is an ego trip, and accepting God's grace requires death of the ego. We humans really like to feel good about ourselves—in fact the essence of fallen human nature is self-exaltation. When we received the stamp of Satan's character in the Garden, mankind downloaded his software program of pride. The obsession of each of us, left to ourselves, is to build up self until we are " ' "like the Most High" ' " (Isaiah 14:14).

We do this by putting God in a position of debt to us, as in Romans 4:4, "Now to him who works, the wages are not counted as grace but as debt" (NKJV). When I work for my salvation, I perceive God as owing me salvation; therefore I feel entitled and worthy. This leads to a blasphemous role reversal where God is subject to man, for "the borrower [God, because in works religion I think He owes me something] is servant to the lender [me, because I think I lent Him my works and therefore have equity with Him]" (Proverbs 22:7, NKJV). Rather, the covenant of grace produces this realization: " 'Who has known the mind of the Lord? Or who has become His counselor? Or who has first given to Him (God) and it shall be repaid to him (man)?' " (Romans 11:34, 35, NKJV).

Receiving God's grace requires me to completely stop playing God with God. Rather, my heart is contrite as I take the gift of God in His Son. Knowing that I am unworthy makes me humble, and knowing He has given me salvation as a free gift makes me grateful. My heart is changed. Instead of constantly trying to establish my own righteousness and living in fear, I receive His righteousness and live in full assurance. The transformation of the motives of my heart produce a change in my character and eventually works of obedience that beautify my life and bring honor to Him.

The Faith of Devils?

Salvation by grace is much more than a legal transaction that blots out my criminal record. It is a life-transforming reality that changes my status and my heart simultaneously. Waggoner loved to harp on the dynamic power of faith. Hear him out for a moment:

> Faith enables one to do that which he is unable to do otherwise. It is not a substitute for work, but it works.[2]
>
> Forgiveness of sins is a reality; it is something tangible, something that vitally affects the individual. It actually clears him from guilt; and if he is cleared from guilt, is justified, made righteous, he has certainly undergone a radical change.[3]

The covenant of salvation by grace through faith is scary to some because it seems like an easy street religion. In reality, it requires more effort and self-scrutiny than salvation by works. "Examine yourselves as to whether you are in the *faith*" (2 Corinthians 13:5, NKJV, emphasis mine). God is so confident that it *will* produce works that He bases His final judgment of us on works (see Matthew 25:31-46; 1 Peter 1:17; Matthew 16:27; 2 Corinthians 11:15). Even if the one who believed had little time and opportunity to manifest their faith in works, as in the case of the thief on the cross (and hopefully my father), the "work" of believing (see John 6:29) stands in the judgment as evidence that other works will follow. In fact, the words of the thief (and perhaps the tears of my dad) were "works" in the sense that they were the fruit of faith, albeit fruit that was limited by circumstances. In the matter of bringing life transformation, God has no doubt that faith will do it. In short, God has faith in faith.

Those of us who regard salvation by grace as a merely legal exchange and not a life-changing force are in danger of adopting a counterfeit for true faith, which is mental assent. It may help to realize that when we embrace such a thing we have the same type of "faith" that the devils have. Remember, "even the demons *believe*—and tremble!" (James 2:19, NKJV, emphasis mine). The devils prove that an acknowledgment of the facts of the Bible can exist in a completely lost soul. But when we speak of saving faith, we are not talking about an acknowledgment of facts, we are talking about a transforming power that etches the character of Christ into our lives. Mental assent faith is not true, saving faith any more than devils are church members in good and regular standing.

"Faith is the substance of things hoped for, the evidence of things not seen" (Hebrews 11:1, NKJV). God can save imperfect people who exercise saving faith on the basis that faith will produce perfect obedience in the end. Immature Christians, given enough time and opportunity, will eventually become mature Christians, provided they do not resist the movings of God's Spirit in their lives. God knows this, and because He has so much confidence in the dynamics He has set in motion, He saves people based on the substance and evidence of faith.

The devil has an accusation against God. "You are taking self-centered human beings into heaven," he says, "and leaving me out for the same sin of selfishness! Unfair!" In order to vindicate Himself, God will, in the end of time, present a people whose faith has come to complete maturity. The very motives of their beings will have been completely overhauled by God's grace, and they will come to the place where they would rather die than sin against Him. It will be seen that God's program of salvation by grace through faith is not a compromise of justice, nor does it lead to disobedience, but rather it establishes justice and produces perfect conformity to His will.

At that time there will be but two categories of people; those who abide by the covenant of grace and those who would prefer to be saved by their own works. Jesus spoke of them as "sheep" and "goats." (See Matthew 25:31-46.)

The sheep will embrace the covenant initiated by God with Abraham, the terms of which are "believe and live."

The goats will embrace the covenant initiated by man at Sinai, the terms of which are "obey and live." (See *Patriarchs and Prophets,* page 372.)

The sheep will humbly believe God's promises to them.

The goats will boastfully make promises to God.

The sheep will receive, by faith, the gift of Christ's righteousness, of which they know they are unworthy.

The goats will manufacture, through their own works, a self-righteousness, which they feel they have earned.

The sheep will know they are indebted to God, and will have a heartfelt gratitude to Him.

The goats will feel that God is indebted to them, and will have a deep-seated contempt for Him.

The sheep will desire, because of their gratitude, to become channels of God's goodness to the world.

The goats will desire, because of their contempt, to oppress their fellow man.

The sheep will eventually have a perfect obedience that springs from a transformed life.

The goats will immediately have a forced obedience that is purely external.

The sheep will be judged righteous because they believed, and faith worked, producing acts of self-giving love toward the needy ones around them, fitting them for a holy heaven.

The goats will be judged unrighteous because they did not believe and their unbelief led them to live lives of supreme self-concern, making them wholly unfit for a selfless heaven.

Can you see the relationship between the covenant of grace and true, heartfelt obedience in the life? Conversely, can you see how the covenant of works actually leads to the *breaking* of God's law of love? Regardless of the myriad of religions and the confusing winds of doctrine all around us, we have only two options. What will it be, grace or works? Humility or pride? Love or contempt? Heaven or hell?

------

1. Lexical Aids to the Old Testament, The Hebrew-Greek Key Study Bible, AMG Publishers, page. 1716.

2. E. J. Waggoner, *The Signs of the Times,* May 8, 1893.

3. E. J. Waggoner, *Christ and His Righteousness,* page. 74.

CHAPTER ELEVEN

Sweet
Forgiveness

Betrayal. The word carries the venom of shock and dismay in its very pronunciation. I know what the word means, not just technically but experientially. Betrayal is when your desire for trust is overwritten by another's heartless disregard of it. Betrayal feels like an unseen knife suddenly sliding into your back and severing your internal parts from one another. Betrayal leaves a wound so raw and profusely bleeding that only the balm of heaven will heal it.

Forgiveness is that balm. Forgiveness rolls off the tongue in a completely opposite way, implying a reverse of damage done. Oh, for the gift of forgiveness in my life! So many blessings have fallen around me unperceived because of the distracting curse of resentment. I realize that I have but two choices when faced with cause for offense—to be a conveyor of God's forgiveness or a vessel of wrath.

I remember one the worst betrayals of my life. The nature of it was so private and personal that, as open as I am, I can't talk about it. Suffice it to say that it left me quite devastated. What made it so hard to bear was the depth of trust I had in this individual to begin with. Deep trust means deep pain when trust is broken. Michael Card put it into words for me one day as I was listening to his song "Why?":

"Only a friend can betray a friend, a stranger has nothing to gain

And only a friend comes close enough to ever cause so much pain."[1]

I had let a "friend" come close, and it caused "so much pain"! Once the damage was done, I struggled to process my feelings. What would I do with this sense of unfinished business, this lack of closure? The person did not even admit that they had done anything wrong, so far be it from them to apologize. I was left with a sore in my heart that was quickly becoming infected with bitterness. I began to realize I needed to forgive, but my human attempts at bestowing forgiveness always resulted in a sentimental, surface "reconciliation" with the person, who would soon relapse into old patterns. The hurtful behavior would begin again, and again I would find myself nursing a lump of animosity. Finally, I was out of ideas, and I decided to search out what God said about forgiveness. The sting of betrayal I couldn't avoid, but the bite of bitterness I could. One way or another, I would forgive, for God's sake, my betrayer's sake, and my own sake.

The passage I centered on was in the "forgiveness chapter," Matthew 18. This chapter has invaluable instruction on how to effect reconciliation in troubled relationships. After giving specific instructions in how to conquer the effects of interpersonal sin and alienation, Jesus drives home the need to maintain an *attitude* of forgiveness toward those who wrong us. It is when we go forward with this attitude in place that our efforts to reconcile with a brother or sister are truly effective. We have all had the experience of someone lambasting us for our sins, and it results in making our hearts more estranged than ever. Thank God there is a better way:

> No one has ever been reclaimed from a wrong position by censure and reproach; but many have thus been driven from Christ and led to seal their hearts against conviction. A tender spirit, a gentle, winning deportment, may save the erring and hide a multitude of sins.[1]

At the end of Matthew 18 was a parable that spoke volumes to me of how to maintain this spirit of forgiveness. It is a simple story:

A king found that one of his property managers owed him ten million dollars. When the manager could not pay, the king threatened to have him incarcerated, but the man pled for time to repay him. Instead, the king forgave him completely. The manager was not so kind, however, to his own debtor, who owed him only twenty dollars. When the manager threw his friend in jail, others heard about his merciless action, and told the king. The manager ended up not just losing his freedom, but being "delivered to the tormentors."

I wasn't sure what "delivered to the tormentors" meant, but it sure sounded bad. After showing the dark destiny of an unforgiving person, Jesus ended with these solemn words:

> "So My heavenly Father also will do to you if each of you, from his heart, does not forgive his brother his trespasses" (Matthew 18:35, NKJV).

I shuddered, realizing that although harboring bitterness put me in danger of losing my own salvation, I couldn't possibly manufacture forgiveness within myself. One thought gave me hope; I knew that my own "feelings and dealings" with people were molded by what I perceived to be God's "feelings and dealings" with me. Maybe there was a flaw somewhere in my God-concept that halted the flow of His grace into my life. I set out to answer the question, "How does God forgive?"

Proactive Pardon

What I discovered was that God's forgiveness is proactive. What this means is that like love, it is "not provoked," not *re*active. When someone seeks God's forgiveness, it is not suddenly created within Him by their repentance, but He bestows forgiveness upon them that existed *before* they repented.

The evidences for this are numerous. The king's forgiveness of the property manager was said to symbolize "divine forgiveness of all sin."[2] Jesus said of the Roman soldiers who nailed him to the cross, " 'Father, forgive them, for they do not know what they do'" (Luke 23:34, NKJV). This prayer "embraced the world"[3] and was reflected in the prayer of the first Christian martyr Stephen, who, while he was being stoned to death said, " 'Lord, do not charge them with this sin' " (Acts 7:60, NKJV). All of these vignettes depicted a God who holds forgiveness the moment a sin is born.

I concluded that God maintains forgiveness toward us at all times. Was I alone in my beliefs? No. Many years before God had shown His 1888 messenger the same thing:

> God is not a man; He does not cherish enmity, nor harbor a feeling of revenge. It is not because He has a hard feeling in His own heart against a sinner that He forgives him, but because the sinner has something in his heart. [4]

I struggled with two images of God. One waited with arms folded and foot tapping impatiently until I came crawling, then, moved by my humiliation, had a change of heart toward me. A second image that was just starting to clarify itself in my mind was of a God who stood anxious to forgive, only withholding forgiveness because He could not find receivers. The latter seemed much more in harmony with the character of God presented repeatedly in the Bible.

On the surface, this seems to conflict with some inspired passages. John 1:9 says, "*If* we confess our sins, He is faithful and just to forgive us our sins . . ." (NKJV, emphasis mine). This seems to say that God does not forgive until we confess. For me, the conflict was resolved when I saw the two-phase aspect of forgiveness. The first phase exists as an unshakable reality within God, and might be called the "objective" phase, meaning that it exists apart from human action. The second phase involves God's forgiveness being received by the penitent, and might be called the "subjective" phase, meaning that it requires human choice. It can be said that God forgives me *before* I repent, but it can also be said that He forgives me *when* I repent. The conditions to receiving forgiveness, confession, and repentance prepare me to receive it rather than persuading God to give it.

This change of thinking helped me resolve the issue of blasphemy against the Holy Spirit. I recalled a tattooed, hardened man that once began to come into my circle of friends. He wanted to be a Christian but was plagued by fears that he had committed the unpardonable sin. No one, including myself, had the guts to ask him what it was that he did, and we were kind of stunned by his anguish, not knowing what to say except "pray harder." To this he would respond by quoting Mark 3:29 over and over, " 'But he who blasphemes against the Holy Spirit *never* has forgiveness' " (NKJV, emphasis mine)!

As I restudied the issue of forgiveness I wished I could find that man. To blaspheme against the Holy Spirit, I saw, was essentially to reject the Spirit's efforts to bring us to conviction and repentance. If we did not see a need for forgiveness, we would not seek it. "Who needs forgiveness?" the blasphemer says, "I haven't done anything wrong!" Therefore, the only sin that a sinner *could not* be forgiven for was the one they *would not* be forgiven. No sin is too great for God to forgive, but even a small sin God will not forgive by force.

The two-phase process applies to other aspects of the relationship between God and man and is the key to many "big words" in the Bible, including "reconciliation" and "adoption," two that we will look at now.

Reconciliation

In 2 Corinthians 5:18 we are told that God has "*reconciled* us to Himself through Jesus Christ" (emphasis mine). A few verses later, we are told to "be *reconciled* to God" (v. 20, emphasis mine), as if we had never been reconciled in the first place! Why the double-talk? Because there is a double phase to reconciliation; a phase that occurs "in Christ"— "through Jesus Christ" as the passage says—and a phase that occurs in *us*.

Two thousand years ago the broken law stood as a barrier between us and God until Jesus paid the price for the transgression of it. Standing in for man as the Second Adam, Jesus effected full reconciliation. But a problem remained in that the heart of man was still estranged from God. Although the first phase of reconciliation was complete— we were reconciled to God in Christ, the second phase had yet to be accomplished—reconciliation to God within ourselves.

All the divine groundwork laid will not *complete* the process of reconciliation unless we respond to God's gracious provision. It is as if God, our estranged Lover, to whom we have served divorce papers, leaves us not just a dozen roses, but a thousand roses, each bright bud representing a drop of Christ's blood. Attached to the bouquet is a note reconfirming His desire to remain espoused to us, entreating us to receive Him. Are we reconciled to Him? As far as *He* is concerned we are, but our hearts may remain alienated even while surrounded with a field of proof that He has suffered infinitely in order to effect peace.

Adoption

Let's warm the concept up a little by using a more relational, less abstract term—adoption. Picture a darling orphan child with a smudged face and growling stomach. A husband and wife fall in love with a photo of the child and decide to adopt her. Legal proceedings begin, requiring hours of tedious questioning and preparation; papers are processed, interviews held, questions asked, and large fees paid (thirty thousand dollars is the going rate). Finally, the adoption is legal and the parents welcome their precious child. As she grows, however, the child begins to exhibit a rebellious streak, and taxes the patience of the parents until they are ready to despair. Finally, one day, the child shouts, "I hate you! I never want to see you again!" and storms out of their lives.

Did those parents do all they could to make the child their own? Yes, they met the legal demands fully at great personal sacrifice. Was the child really theirs? Yes, in two places the child was theirs; on paper (legally) and in their own hearts. In the same way, God "predestined us to adoption as sons through Jesus Christ to Himself" (Ephesians 1:5). The legal requirements of adoption were fully met before we were even born, for "he chose us in Him before the foundation of the world" (v. 4).

However, when the child stormed out of the parents' lives, she was, by her own decree, no longer theirs. In the same way, we declare ourselves unrelated to God through persistent rejection of Him. In the final reckoning, it will be seen that God did not ultimately reject anyone, rather, the lost rejected *Him* until finally He accepted his or her decision to reject Him.

God has adopted us, each and every one. His heart is infinitely large, able to hold every human being within it as His own child, but in order for bonding to be complete between the Parent and child, the child must ultimately want it as well. The child must choose to, in heart, make the Parent their own, or the contract will ultimately be shattered, not by the Parent, but by the child itself. In Heaven's adoption of humanity, God made the first overture, but the answering chord must be struck within the heart of humanity before the masterpiece is complete.

Can you see the pattern here? Jesus has brought humanity and Heaven back into harmony with one another by first harmonizing them within Himself. "God with us" was only possible because God was first with Him who lived *as* us.

In becoming one with us, Jesus forgave the condemned, reconciled the alienated, and adopted the orphaned. This is why it was necessary for Him to take upon Himself our fallen human nature—it was fallen humanity He came to save, not the unfallen. "For indeed He does not give aid to angels, but He does give aid to the seed of Abraham" (Hebrews 2:16, NKJV). Once He took our sin upon Him in the form of our sinful nature and lived a perfect life in it, He completed that process by taking that same sin upon Him at the Cross where He exhausted the penalty for it. And all this was done completely without my consent or permission, apart from my choice. All this was done "in Christ." I can add nothing to it and take nothing away from it. It is a done deal whether I like it or not. But I like it. Do you?

I am saddened when I hear people say the following: "If I do not receive Christ, His sacrifice does me NO GOOD!" How can we say such a thing while we live and breathe "in Him" (Acts 17:28)? Failing to acknowledge all that Christ has already achieved for us results in the most blatant form of ingratitude.

This is the distinguishing mark of the gospel. If God is the Initiator of the process of forgiveness, reconciliation, and adoption, laying the groundwork at great sacrifice to Himself, then it is truly "good news." If man initiates the process of forgiveness, reconciliation and adoption, it is not "good news" but "good advice" telling us to do something to improve our situation. When man becomes the initiator of the process of salvation, legalism results and the purity of the gospel is compromised.

Forgiveness Applied

After several days of immersing myself in the study of forgiveness, I emerged ready to try again. This time, however, I learned that the forgiveness needed to be in place within myself before I approached the person and attempted reconciliation. This forgiveness was based upon and fueled by God's forgiveness toward me, not the repentance of the individual, and so it was stable and changeless.

Interestingly, the ability to forgive this individual resulted in my being able to form proper boundaries. I had previously confused forgiveness and trust and assumed that once I forgave the person, I was obligated to trust again. But now I saw that forgiveness existed apart from the person changing, I could forgive them even before they proved I could trust them. Ultimately, the goal of reconciliation is the re-establishment of the relationship, but this comes later and is contingent upon the person earning back the confidence of the one wronged. Unfortunately, in my circumstance, the person never came out of denial long enough to admit their fault, so the relationship was never restored (at least not yet!). I was, however, able to forgive them from the heart and in so doing detach from the relationship.

Once again God had released, through difficulties, a key that unlocked the beauty of the gospel to my understanding. This comprehension of forgiveness has helped equip me to deal with many conflicts and interpersonal struggles that have come since that time. God did not wait for me to make the first move in reconciliation, but He initiated and even completed the work in Christ. "When we were enemies, we were reconciled to God through the death of His Son" (Romans 5:10, NKJV).

Now I can, like Him, be an initiator in the process of reconciliation by following His advice: " 'Whenever you stand praying, if you have anything against anyone, forgive him . . .' " (Mark 11:25, NKJV). I should lose my grudges and keep an environment of forgiveness in my heart, He is saying. Certainly I can assume He does the same.[5]

> In Christianity, God seeks elusive man to bestow forgiveness, and man responds with a change of heart toward God.
> In legalism, man seeks an elusive God to obtain forgiveness, and God responds with a change of heart toward man.

> In Christianity, God begins the process of reconciliation, and man completes it by saying "yes" to God.
> In legalism, man begins the process of reconciliation, and God completes it by saying "yes" to man.

> In Christianity, God is the Great Initiator, adopting man while man is estranged from Him.

In legalism, man is the great initiator, seeking to be adopted by God while God is estranged from him.

---

1. Card, Michael, "Why?" in his CD, *Brother to Brother,* or *Joy in Journey,* 1984, Mole End Music.

2. Ellen White, *Thoughts From the Mount of Blessing,* page 128.

3. Ellen White, *Christ's Object Lessons,* page 244.

4. Ellen White, *The Desire of Ages,* page 745.

5. E.J. Waggoner, "The Power of Forgiveness," *The Signs of the Times,* April 10, 1893.

6. *"We should not think that unless those who have injured us confess the wrong we are justified in withholding from them our forgiveness. It is their part, no doubt, to humble their hearts by repentance and confession; but we are to have a spirit of compassion toward those who have trespassed against us, whether or not they confess their faults."* Ellen White, *Thoughts from the Mount of Blessing,* pages 113 and 114.

CHAPTER TWELVE

"You Are No Better"

One of my least favorite things under the sun is a marriage seminar. My apologies to those who conduct them, but there's something so contrary about the forum itself that I have a hard time being open to anything the presenters might say, however valuable. What I am speaking of is the premise that people can learn, in a carefully controlled setting, techniques that will enable two sinners to intertwine their lives in anything but a chaotic knot. Little love notes in the lunch box. Twelve meaningful touches a day. Fighting fair. See-through nighties (a pastor, yes, a pastor, recommended that one in front of a huge crowd). How can something as manmade as a *technique* undertake something as supernatural as a permanent spiritual union? Sorry, I'm a bit cynical.

I once watched some friends present a method that helped them. They looked so sparkling up there in front, and I felt so grubby in contrast. I appreciated this couple's commitment to each other, but their marriage was young, and they had no children and far fewer financial pressures than we did. Another presentation by a man included sighs and romantic remarks about his method of courting his absolutely gorgeous wife. I couldn't help but feel for all the "average" people sitting there (including me) who were extrapolating that they could never have such bliss because they didn't have such looks. Yet another man spoke of his affectionate treatment of his wife in very white-knightly terms until I sensed that the woman there, most of whom were without their husbands because the fellows didn't care to be white-knighted, were starting to wish they were married to *him*. In all of these scenarios, I failed to get the help intended because I believed that these people somehow had superior equipment to mine, that their marriage worked because they were just intrinsically happier. The more "encouragement" I got from these "good" marriages, the less accessible a "good" marriage became.

What finally made sense for me was to discard the idea that there is such a thing as a good marriage. Anecdotal evidence proved me right when marriages I had always considered strong unraveled before my eyes or began to manifest gaping holes. Then there were the ones I thought would never make it still putt-putting along after decades. My own might be included in that category. Neither my husband nor I have ever entertained the idea of legal divorce, but we have had a few psychological divorces over the years. It seems, however, that we have hung together better with the glue of adversity than we would have with the threads of ease. God is faithful.

A marriage is only as "good" as the people who comprise it, and the Lord has the final word on human goodness, which is that there is no such thing. "There is none who does good, no, not one" (Psalm 14:3, NKJV). But although no person is good, grace through faith can transform him or her. In the same way, although no marriage is good, faith can transform *it*. In the end, what we *believe* impacts more upon the shape of ourselves and our marriages than what we do. Not that behaviors aren't important, but behaviors have their origin in beliefs, so behavior modification is best served by thought modification.

Disassociation or Identification?

There is one belief that above all others has steered my marriage into a healthier, happier mode than it would have had otherwise. It is hard, however, to tell you what it is. In so doing, I will have to admit my own spiritual downfall. So bear with me while I get up the nerve to say it.

Although there are many fancy theological terms for this belief, I find that stating it in a few simple words is the most helpful. God spoke these words to me, not audibly, but in moment of revelation, a moment which duplicates itself almost daily. They hit me hard:

"You are no better than him."

The core belief that needed to be routed out of my thinking was that I was somehow superior to my spouse, that I was the big one in the marriage, the martyr, the saint, and he was the bad guy. This thinking made me feel virtuous for a time, but when the pleasure of feeling saintly confronted the pain of feeling cheated, the pain won out and I began to sulk.

One of the things that makes this stinking thinking possible is the fact that sin comes in a variety pack. A wife has one variety, while her spouse has another. I suppose in this sense my husband and I were the personification of the adage that "opposites attract" in that we didn't even have similar *sins*. When I wanted to win an argument, I would look at his sins and feel very self-righteous indeed because I didn't fall on those points. That was all well and good until he did the same thing and looked at my sins, which he wasn't tempted by at all. When *he* then felt self-righteous, there were two people under the same roof feeling holier-than-thou, and let me assure you, there is a no more miserable state of existence.

Honesty about our total lack of righteousness is a better option.

Alcoholism was an incurable disease until the inception of AA. Much of its success is due to the fact that the individuals that meet all have the same addiction, and therefore no one is able to feel superior to those around him or her. No drunk can say of another's drunken binge, "I would never do that!"—their very presence at AA is an admission that they would! In this environment of honesty, progress can be made toward healing.

It is God's will that the church foster that same kind of honesty. While each have their distinctive struggles, there should be a recognition that "all have sinned and fall short of the glory of God" (Romans 3:23). The problem is, our distance vision is good enough to see the sins of those far away from us, but "presbeopia"* blurs things right in front of our eyes, such as our own shortcomings. This is why we need " ' "eye salve . . . that [we] may see" ' " (Revelation 3:18).

It is ironic that self-righteousness had its nativity in the first marriage on planet Earth (marriage ever since then has proven to be a perfect breeding ground for it). Adam and Eve, when they began to realize their lost condition, clothed themselves with fig leaves that represent "the arguments used to cover disobedience."[1] They had never known guilt, and now it threatened to engulf them. They then did what human beings typically do to deflect guilt—they manufactured their own righteousness.

I can't blame them, for guilt is a deadly thing. In fact, it was our guilt that crushed out the life of Jesus on the cross when He was "slain by the sin of the world."[2] No one in their right mind wants to walk into the jaws of condemnation without the armor of righteousness. We can't! Human beings are created with a powerful self-preservation instinct that will cause us to avoid what will destroy us, including self-annihilating guilt. So we must have righteousness from some source, and in the absence of Christ's righteousness we will contrive our own.

Now, watch what happened to the original marriage. Once they fig-leafed their own righteousness, they began to blame one another, for when we attempt to ward off blame it must go somewhere. When God finally confronted them, their relationship had completely disintegrated. Remember, Adam thought that God was coming to destroy him and in so doing fulfill His vow that " 'in the day that you eat of it you shall surely die' " (Genesis 2:17, NKJV). When Adam was sure he was about to be executed, he attempted to hoodwink the Lord into thinking that Eve was the culprit, hoping that God would execute her and spare him. Only hours before Adam had "loved" Eve so much that he chose to sell the creation into the hands of the serpent in order to remain with her. Where was that love when he blamed her for his sin? Gone, because the desire to be with her was subsumed by the desire to survive.

The same survival instinct leads us to go to outrageous lengths in order to defend our own righteousness and avoid deadly guilt. To do this we put the high beam on the sins of others, as Adam spotlighted the sin of his wife (the trend continues to this day). This produces a temporary sense of freedom from blame, but no lasting peace.

When we are faced with sin in the lives of friends, enemies, and spouses (which can be either), we can have one of two reactions: disassociation or identity. Disassociation leads us to express shock, "Gasp! They did *that?*" The sentiment behind the shock is, "I would never do that! I can't even relate to it!" A better reaction is to follow God's advice, " 'Sigh, therefore, son of man, *with a breaking heart,* and sigh with bitterness before their eyes' " (Ezekiel 21:6, NKJV, emphasis mine). God would have us identify *with a breaking heart* with the sin, as if it was our own, on the basis that it could be.

But the typical reaction is an alarm that implies self-righteousness. Do you have this problem? I do. Thank God He has shown me the following:

> What I disassociate from I will eventually do.
> The best thing for me to do then, in the light of this fact is:
> Admit that I am capable of anything.

Jesus spells out this disassociation syndrome for us in Matthew 23:29-36. He pointed out to the religious leaders of the day that they would " 'build the tombs of the prophets and adorn the monuments of the righteous' " and claim that, " ' "If we had lived in the days of our fathers, we would not have been partakers with them in the blood of the prophets." ' " Jesus then said, " 'you are witnesses against yourselves' " and told them to " 'fill up, then, the measure of your fathers' guilt' " (NKJV), after which He predicts that they will indeed kill, crucify, and scourge the prophets, scribes, and wise men that He sends to them.

Here's the point. There was an inextricable link between their denial of their fathers' sins and their repetition of them. Scribes, Pharisees: What you disassociate from, you will eventually do. Admit that you are capable of anything.

Righteous persons fall short because of their ignorance of these realities. Gideon defeated Midian but manifested a spirit of retaliation toward some neutral cities (Judges 8:16, 17) and eventually led Israel into idolatry (vs. 26, 27). Jehu was mightily used of God in eradicating Baal worship from Israel, but never quite left idolatry himself (2 Kings 10:31). King Josiah was a great reformer in Judah and Jerusalem but would not listen to a heathen king when God spoke through him, resulting in his own death (2 Chronicles 35:20-22). These men were used of God to root out sin but were finally found to have the same sins themselves. Perhaps this is because they didn't recognize within themselves the potential to do just what the recipients of their judgment did.

Gideon, Jehu, Josiah: What you disassociate from, you will eventually do. Admit that you are capable of anything.

Our Collective Identity

On what basis can we admit that we are capable of anything? On the basis that all human beings share the same fallen human nature, which at its worst will murder God Himself. True, some of us "act out" the evil of our natures more than others, but all have the same basic tendency to exalt self over God.

If we are all the same in nature, why do some seem so given over to evil and some so basically good? Because each of us are a composite of three factors:

1. Genetics
2. Environment
3. Choices

While every one of us is born with a self-centered nature, that nature expresses itself in ways that are molded by these three factors. Our genes and environment dictate every tendency from arrogance to alcoholism. Our choices can either lessen or reinforce these tendencies. Of the three factors listed above, the first two are inherited, meaning that we had no choice in them (environment refers to the growing up years). The third factor, choice, is something we do have some say in, but only present choices, as our past mistakes have already been made.

No one would argue that all have the same advantages. Clearly, a child raised in a loving, intact family who came from a long line of well-adjusted people has an advantage over a child raised in an alcoholic, abusive home with the blight of death all over the family tree. But take sin outside of the realm of society and church where it is sorted and labeled, and all sin is seen as being the same in essence. Even the "lesser sin" of "the better person" will eventually degenerate into the worst sin if left unchecked. Every sin if taken to its nth degree is murder of God.

Part of our inability to comprehend this principle comes from the individualism that characterizes Western thinking. We tend to see humans as separate entities. We look at those with the worst sins and think ourselves apart from them. As community is de-prioritized and selfhood is increasingly celebrated in our society, our Western minds find it hard to grasp the idea of a corporate soul. The Bible, however, presents humanity in both individualistic and corporate terms. While humans are presented as *individually* responsible for their personal choices, they are also seen as *communally* responsible for their group choices.

The biblical principle of headship moves us toward recognition of group identity. In biblical times, the head of a family or race was seen to *contain* those who were members, even before they were born. Examples of this are numerous. Here are a few:

> Abraham lied to the heathen king Abimelech, saying that Sarah was his sister. The king took Sarah as his wife, and in so doing, nearly incurred the judgment of God upon himself. Abimelech's response to God's death threat was, "Lord, wilt Thou slay a *nation*?" (Genesis 20:4, NASB, emphasis mine). The entire nation of Gerar was in Abimelech.

> Abraham paid tithes to the mysterious priest Melchizedek after defeating the kings who attacked Sodom. The Levitical priesthood was said to pay tithes through Abraham at this time, because Levi "was still in the loins of his father when Melchizedek met him" (Hebrews 7:10, 11). The entire priesthood was in Abraham, even though unborn (see Genesis 14).

> As Rebekah struggled to give birth to Jacob and Esau, she was told that, " 'Two nations are in your womb' " (Genesis 25:23). The entire nations of Israel and Edom were encapsulated in her unborn twins.

We would do well to readjust our Western thinking to include this ancient awareness that man has both an individuality and a solidarity. Especially as we endeavor to deal with one another's shortcomings do we need a keen awareness that *"All* we like sheep have gone astray" (Isaiah 53:6, NKJV, emphasis mine). I may not have committed the same sins as my brother, but on the basis of the fact that I possess the same fallen nature as he, I may identify with his failure because I identify with the corporate failure of humanity.

On a practical level, this identity and honesty makes the body of believers to facilitate healing of individuals. No longer do we have to maintain a facade of righteousness—the knowledge of our oneness has let the cat out of the bag. We are all sinners, saved by grace alone, and this understanding brings us out of isolation into fellowship. Isolation breeds spiritual weakness, but fellowship breeds strength, which is why we are told that:

4—M.P.M.

Two are better than one, because they have a good reward for their labor. For if they fall, one will lift up his companion. But who to him who is alone when he falls, for he has no one to help him up. Again, if two lie down together, they will keep warm; but how can one be warm alone? Though one may be overpowered by another, two can withstand him. And a three-fold cord is not quickly broken (Ecclesiastes 4:9-12, NKJV).

This mind-bending concept of collective identity was an essential ingredient of the 1888 message. Listen to Waggoner use it as a spring-board for his teaching on our dealings with fellow sinners:

Since all men are alike sharers in one common human na-ture, it is evident that whosoever in the world condemns another for any misdeed thereby condemns himself; for the truth is that all have the same evil in them, more or less fully developed. . . .[3]

At the foot of the Cross is a level playing field where none can boast, for all must look up and see the One they crucified. This place where no self-exaltation can flourish is exactly where the delicate plant of love can thrive between human beings.

Does this understanding rule out accountability? Should I totally ignore sin in others because I recognize my capability to commit the same? No, in fact, the recognition of my own potential is the only thing that gives me the proper basis to confront sin in others.

"Brethren, if a man is overtaken in any trespass, you who are spiritual restore such a one in a spirit of gentleness, considering yourself lest you also be tempted" (Galatians 6:1, NKJV).

Notice that my motive is to "restore such a one." By ignoring serious sin in the lives of those within my influence, I am missing an opportunity to *restore* them. Rather, Jesus would have us seek the deliverance of those for whom He died. But we are to do it in a "spirit of gentleness," divested of the least hint of self-righteousness, that our desire to help might shine through to their hearts. It is the opposite approach, the mean-spirited approach, that has made us afraid to address the sin problem at all—we think that condemnation and judgmentalism are intrinsic to the act of going to one who is "over-taken."

Our relationships suffer because our thinking is saturated with rugged individualism that caters to self-righteousness. We would all do well to expand that thinking to include a corporate identity with our fellow sinners. Once we can look at each and every person and say, "I am no better than him," we will be in a position to understand and appreciate, to empathize and help, and finally, to love and cherish.

Marriage seminars? Actually, I have heard good things about them. I know people who have been greatly helped and blessed. I repent for my bad attitude! But I maintain my belief that what we *think* is more foundational to a good marriage than what we do. And God has changed my thoughts. He has convinced me that in essence, I am no different than my spouse. Strangely, this has made all the difference in the world.

Christ's righteousness leads me to realize that I am the chief of sinners.

Self-righteousness leads me to feel holier-than-thou.

Christ's righteousness gives me permission to be honest about my sinfulness.

Self-righteousness gives me incentive to lie about my goodness.

Christ's righteousness leads me to release guilt as I confess my sin.

Self-righteousness leads me to avoid guilt as I cover up my sin.

Christ's righteousness leads me to lay down my life as He laid down His.

Self-righteousness leads me to go to great lengths in self-preservation.

Christ's righteousness causes me to identify with the sins of others, knowing that I am capable of the same.

Self-righteousness compels me to disassociate from the sins of others, thinking that I am *not* capable of the same.

Christ's righteousness motivates me to lovingly seek the restoration of those who have fallen.

Self-righteousness leads me to either ignore or censure those who have fallen.

Christ's righteousness makes me see myself as part of collective humanity.

Self-righteousness makes me see myself as merely an individual.

Christ's righteousness is received at the foot of the cross.

Self-righteousness is expressed by nailing Jesus there.

---

* Presbeopia is what happens to old people's eyes (old meaning over forty, which I am) where they can't read close up anymore, and they say, "I'm not getting older, my arms are just getting shorter!" then finally go buy those fifteen-dollar reading glasses from Wal-Mart.

1. Ellen White, *Review and Herald,* June 4, 1901.

2. Ellen White, *The Desire of Ages,* page 772.

3. Ellet Waggoner, *Waggoner On Romans,* 2.39, 2.40.

CHAPTER THIRTEEN

Absolute Salvation? Absolutely!

If a tree fell in the woods and no one was there to hear it, would it make a sound?

Pardon me, but I think that's a dumb question.

I can recall my philosophy teachers posing it as if the answer might actually be "no." In just entertaining that possibility they were implying something completely opposed to Christianity and even rational thought. They were saying that a human being's perception may be the thing that determines whether something is real or not. If the tree *didn't* make a sound because no one was there to hear it, then human ears are what determine sound. Obviously, this is atheistic in that it denies the omnipresence of a God who hears everything. But the converse of this philosophy is even more godless; if something isn't real unless a human perceives it, then something *is* real just by virtue of the fact that it *is* perceived by a human. Perceptions determine fact! There are no absolutes! Create your own reality!

What a bunch of anthropocentric mumbo-jumbo.

Why am I talking about this? Because the ideas outlined above have infiltrated Western thinking in the last thirty years and in the process have attempted to wipe Christianity out of our culture. Humanism, subjectivism, postmodernism—whatever you want to call it—has made a

god out of man by saying that nothing is real except what his perceptions determine is real. But this is not a new way of thinking. Reality, or
truth, has been the special object of the "father of lies" since the beginning of his treason. The lies of Lucifer and the subjectivity of a
postmodernist are the same in essence; instead of bowing to transcen-
dent truth, I make up my own story. Whether I rebel against God or
deny His existence, I resist His claims on my life. Whether I argue with
God's Word or ignore it, I am refusing its influence.

The Bible claims something that shocks the subjective thinker. It
says that there *is* an absolute, unchanging truth that is not contingent
upon our perceptions. Putting the issue in the context of the gospel, we
ask; "If Jesus died and no one believed it, would He still have died for
every soul?" Of course the answer is yes. The tree of Calvary crashed in
the woods of humankind and it *did* make a sound whether anyone heard
it or not (fortunately some did, and more will). The sound it made was
"It is finished!" The work of God in saving humankind was *finished*
when Jesus bowed His sacred head in death.

Part of my journey through the teachings of Jones and Waggoner
included the discovery of the finished work of Christ on the cross. I
began to realize that the salvation Jesus wrought out for me in His life,
death, and resurrection was complete in Him apart from my response.
When I heard and believed in that finished work, I gave it access to my
heart where it could work a dynamic change, but the work itself was not
altered, supplemented, or otherwise tweaked by my believing in it. It
was reality *apart* from my perceptions. Here is how Waggoner said it:

> God has wrought out salvation for every man, and has given
> it to him; but the majority spurn it and throw it away. The judge-
> ment will reveal the fact that full salvation was given to every
> man and that the lost have deliberately thrown away their birth-
> right possession.[1]

If we are to understand the gospel, we must realize that it is something completely objective, meaning that we can't add anything to it or
take anything away from it. "Gospel" is literally *euaggelion,* or "good
news," an already established fact, an unshakable reality. The gospel is
specifically the sacrifice of Christ, for Paul said that the gospel is "the
message of the cross" (1 Corinthians 1:17, 18, NKJV). The holy life

and sacrificial death of Christ is good news for us indeed, for it brings us every blessing we know.

> To the death of Christ we owe even this earthly life. The bread we eat is the purchase of His broken body. The water we drink is bought by His spilled blood.[2]

None of the five major non-Christian religions—Hinduism, Islam, Buddhism, Confucianism, and Judaism—have a gospel in this purest sense of the word. All of them have a way of salvation, but none of them have the good news of a salvation that is already complete. All of them prescribe something that must be done to save oneself, but only the Bible presents the idea that salvation already exists as a free gift to all who will receive it. Since all heresies rest upon the notion that man can save himself, the effect of all false religions, even apostate Christianity, is to deny the richness of all that was accomplished on the cross of Calvary.

We can discern error by whether a teaching stumbles at that " 'stumbling stone,' " (Romans 9:33, NKJV). I put this principle to the test when my sister Kristin was troubled by a friend who got involved in a fanatical group. She felt the lady was wrong and began to pore over her Bible day and night to try to compile enough quotes to refute her ideas. Gradually, Kristin began to think maybe the lady was right based solely on the fact that the lady could "out quote" her. I had received a piece of literature from the same organization and, knowing that all false religions deny the Cross, determined to find something that would settle my sister's mind. Sure enough, there it was on page 7:

> The moment we accept Christ as our Savior, repent, and are baptized, at that very moment all of our trespasses against the Law are blotted out and our penalty paid for by the death and blood of Christ.[3]

This is a serious compromise of the truth cloaked in Christian language! It is saying that we must do something—accept Christ, repent, be baptized—in order for our *penalty to be paid!*

"Does Jesus die again on the cross every time someone comes to Him?" I asked Kristin, who got the point immediately. This fanatical teaching mitigated what Christ had done for the human race by saying the penalty wasn't paid until humans did something first. In a twisted way, it promoted the re-crucifixion of the Son of God with every conversion! This stumbling at the atonement is characteristic of all man-made gospels.

What, Where, and When

What exactly was accomplished at the Cross? This question is so big that I would be a self-inflated fool to claim to know the answer, but I would like to look at the question for a moment anyway. Actually, not a moment, but an eternity, starting now.

> Blessed *be* the God and Father of our Lord Jesus Christ, who has blessed us with every spiritual blessing in the heavenly *places* in Christ, just as He chose us in Him before the foundation of the world, that we should be holy and blameless before Him. In love (Ephesians 1:3, 4).

This passage is speaking of what has come to the human race in Christ. What did we get? "Every spiritual blessing." Where did we get it? "In Christ." *When* did we get it? "Before the foundation of the world." Jesus is the "Lamb slain from the foundation of the world," (Revelation 13:8, NKJV), so we received these things in Christ via the cross of Calvary.

If we received something "in Christ" before the world began, we must have been in Christ before the world began. In what sense can this be true? In the sense that He is the head of the redeemed human race. Recall that in biblical thought the nation or family was encapsulated in the head of that group. The human race is said to be "in Adam," both the first Adam and the Second, which is Christ. "For as in Adam all die, so also in Christ all shall be made alive" (1 Corinthians 15:22). This is very bad news followed by very, very good news.

Bad news first. "For the judgment which came from one offense resulted in condemnation," (Romans 5:16a, NKJV). When Adam fell, the human race was literally inside his procreative faculties—the Bible calls them "loins." Because we were in him, we shared in the bad effects of his choice the way an unborn baby sickens when its mother becomes addicted to cocaine. No one accuses the crack baby of being responsible for their state, but no one denies that they are in a sorry one. We are in a sorry state due to Adam's choice, and that is why we sin, suffer, and die.

Now the good news. "The free gift which came from many offenses resulted in justification" (v. 16b, NKJV). As soon as there was a sin, there was a Savior. Jesus entered the stream of humanity and turned the river back heavenward. In so doing, He became the Second Adam, the representative-head of a new, hope-captive human race.

As we were all in the loins of the first Adam, we are in the spiritual loins of Christ. As we had nothing to do with the first Adam's choice to sin, we had nothing to do with the Last Adam's choice to save.

Let us dwell a little longer upon what we receive in Christ, lest we be guilty of failing to appreciate all He is to us. Let us not say the word "but" even once while we look at these good things, lest we be guilty of trying to fix something that isn't broken. What every man, woman, and child have received "in Christ" is worthy of our unhampered attention. Let's give it.

1. Salvation—Jesus is called the "Savior of all men, especially of those who believe" (1 Timothy 4:10, NKJV). He has saved *all* from the penalty of sin, releasing them from condemnation. The fires of hell were not designed for any human being, but rather for " ' "the devil and his angels" ' " (Matthew 25:41). The gift of salvation came to every human being "in Christ" when Jesus by His atoning death "redeemed Adam's disgraceful fall, and saved the world."[4]

2. Predestination—Saved from condemnation, we are predestined to live in a blissful eternity. " 'When He ascended on high, He led captivity captive' " (Ephesians 4:8, NKJV). We are captive to the hope of heaven! Predestination by definition must plan ("destinate") someone's future before ("pre") they have any input. True, we can refuse our destiny, but other than our own choice, "Who shall separate us from the love of Christ?" (Romans 8:35).

3. Justification—Although the word "justification" is most commonly used in reference to a personal faith experience, it is also one of the spiritual blessings waiting for me "in Christ." The bearing of our sin on the cross was tantamount to justifying us in that it cleared us of the legal penalty of sin. "By His knowledge the Righteous One, My Servant, will *justify* the many, *As He will bear their iniquities*" (Isaiah 53:11, NASB, emphasis mine). Notice that those whose iniquities were borne

were the ones justified. Romans 5:18 is crystal clear that the gift of justification has been poured out on every human being:

> Therefore, as through one man's offense judgement came to all men, resulting in condemnation, even so through one Man's righteous act the free gift came to all men, resulting in justification of life (NKJV).

Waggoner comments:

> As the condemnation came upon all, so the justification comes upon all. Christ has tasted death for every man. He has given Himself for all. Nay, he has given Himself *to* every man. The free gift has come upon all. The fact that it is a free gift is evidence that there is no exception. If it came upon only those who have some special qualification, then it would not be a free gift . . . There is not the slightest reason why every man that has ever lived should not be saved unto eternal life, except that they would not have it. So many spurn the gift offered so freely.[5]

4. Glorification—"Whom He predestined, these He also called; and whom He called, these He also justified; and whom He justified, them He also glorified" (Romans 8:30). This verse tells us that Christ predestined, called, justified, and glorified us. None of us have experienced glorification yet, but in Christ it is a done deal, past tense, old news. But oh, such good news! Don't resist His plan and reject the new, glorified body He has already prepared in the glorification of His own. This verse shows us that *all* the phases of salvation exist before they are experienced in us.

So What?

What practical difference does all this make in Christian experience? Let me tell you how it has impacted me.

I can recall a vague insecurity that came as a result of not ever being sure if I was justified. Once a teacher came through my circle of influence who preached, like most, that justification occurs only when we repent of our sins and receive Christ. She went a step further, though, and maintained that when we sin, we become "unjustified." It then devolves upon us, she said, to immediately repent so that we can again be cleared of condemnation.

While I agreed that it was possible to lose salvation, I saw this on-again-off-again view of justification produce sad results. I knew parents who sheltered their children to an extreme degree and reasoned like this: If my child slips away from my watchful eye and sins, then is suddenly killed, they may die in an unsaved condition. Somehow, this constant fear of damnation seemed out of place for Christians who were supposed to have the peace of God.

We may think this approach is extreme, but what this teacher was doing was taking the logic of human-initiated justification to its conclusion. Our works, which include repentance, confession, and conversion, should be a *response* to what God has already done for us in Christ rather than an attempt to get Him to do it. While these "steps to Christ," are necessary, our deceitful hearts can even make saving works out of *them*. Faith and everything it involves is not our savior, but rather, a channel through which we receive our Savior. If these activities are driven by a desire to persuade God to accept us, they will always be motivated by fear. From this tenuous salvation paradigm comes a proverbial question that you have heard in some form:

> What if Joe Schmoe was working for the phone company and had to climb a ladder to work on the telephone wires. Joe is a Christian, but when his foot slips on the ladder and he bumps his chin on the top rung, he blurts out an expletive. Unfortunately, Joe falls to the ground and dies instantly with no time to repent for cussing. Will he be saved?

This question isn't even worth answering because it makes a tic-tac-toe game out of salvation. It portrays a God who treats people like opponents in a competition, who has created a plan whereby—if they are clever enough and strong enough—they will win. In this view, salvation depends more upon the luck of the draw than the trend of the life. Where does that pathetic picture come from? Certainly not from the One who said,

> He who did not spare His own Son, but delivered Him up for us all, how will He not also with Him freely give us all things? (Romans 8:32).

The Cross speaks with eloquence of God's passion for us—He gave His own Son to save us! In the gift of His Son is the most conclusive proof I should ever require that there is *nothing,* including salvation itself, that God would withhold from me! What more proof do I need? Conjectures in regards to personal salvation so often make God appear willing to revoke it at any moment. How dare we distort Him so when the Gift was given before we ever so much as lifted a prayer?

Some wonder what could possibly convert sinners if they are told that they are saved, predestined, justified, and glorified "in Christ." They see this teaching as bringing with it a false security. I propose two things; one, that we should not consult our finite perceptions regarding what will motivate and then modify our proclamation of truth to fit it; and two, that if a little common sense is used in its presentation, this idea will not fail to motivate. Try this:

> Dear Mr. Sinner, Christ has paid the penalty for your sin and released you from condemnation. He relived all of human history, including yours, and now in Him you stand free of condemnation before God. He has poured upon this world all spiritual blessings including forgiveness, righteousness, and salvation. This is why you have water to drink, food to eat, and life pulsing through your veins. Jesus is asking you to receive this gift of Himself, not just passively in the form of those blessings, but actively by yielding your life to Him. If you do, you will live forever, but if you don't, God will someday leave you to your own choice to be separated from Him, the Source of life. To be seperated from life is to die and to never live again. Life is uncertain. You don't know when your window of opportunity may be forever shut. Receive Christ today, Mr. Sinner. You will never regret it.

God is " 'kind to the unthankful and evil,' " and " 'He makes His sun rise on the evil and on the good, and sends rain on the just and on the unjust' " (Luke 6:35 and Matthew 5:45, NKJV). He can do this because "Christ, the Son of God, stood between the living and the dead, saying, 'Let the punishment fall on Me. I will stand in man's place. He shall have another chance.' "[6] That "other chance," or probation, is ours because of what God did in Christ before I ever had eyes to see it.

But I want to give a little balance now. While the bedrock of my salvation is secure in Christ apart from my response, God would have me respond. The foundation is there, solid and strong, but it isn't God's desire to have a neighborhood full of foundations with nothing upon them. It is Jesus' intense desire that building take place, through faith of course, and yes, with human effort working in cooperation. This is God's ultimate longing. While we don't often see the word "but" after the proclamation of the gospel, we do see the word "that." For instance,

> " 'God so loved the world, that He gave His only begotten Son, *that* whoever believes in Him should not perish, but have eternal life' " (John 3:16, emphasis mine).

"That" indicates God's purpose that the gift of His Son (the gospel) will produce *belief,* which results in *eternal life.* In other words, God's ultimate goal is our eternal salvation, which can only be received through a faith response to the gospel. "That" points to God's goal of awakening within us faith that works by love. How can we refuse to cooperate with His plan? He gutted the vaults of heaven upon one measly planet that He could have snuffed out in a second (speaking in terms of ability, not character). He literally *donated* His only Son to the fallen race after suffering the rending asunder of His own heart when a sin-bearing Jesus was cut off from His holy gaze. He continues to engross Himself in the human saga, mobilizing the armies of heaven moment by moment to coax us one-by-one to receive the Son He could have kept to Himself. And in the face of all this, He asks one small thing—I can almost hear His plaintive tone—"Believe." No, not the "believe" that recites the facts with no heartbrokeness, but the "believe" that falls on its face in worship, then rises to serve with joy. Can you and I be so stone cold as to refuse?

Realizing what God has done for me "in Christ" releases me from the puny insecurities about my own salvation that keep me from truly living for Him. My foundation is not in *me,* it is in *Christ.* I do not repent, confess, and receive Him in order to get Him to receive me. When I see what God has already completed for me "in Christ," my heart is motivated to do all that I do out of gratitude rather than fear. I repent of my sin, not to get into Christ, but out of sorrow for hurting the One who took me into Himself. I confess, not to get into Christ, but out of a desire to be honest with Him who knew me before I knew He did. I receive Christ, not to get into Christ, but because I am honored that He wishes to indwell me. Is there an absolute truth? Yes, and it is Jesus. He has taken us into Himself with the hope that we will take Him into ourselves. There is no better time to start than now.

The good news tells me of a finished work in Christ and inspires me to tell others.

The good advice tells me to finish the work myself and causes me to repel others.

The good news sees Christ's cross in every blessing.

The good advice sees my own cross in every curse.

The good news stands back and appreciates the Cross and all it is to me.

The good advice strides forward and forgets the Cross because of all that needs to be done.

The good news sees salvation as a huge gift.

The good advice sees salvation as a small chance.

The good news believes that there is nothing God would withhold, and so it gives all to Him.

The good advice thinks that God is reluctant to share, and so it holds back from Him.

---

1. E. J. Waggoner, *Glad Tidings,* page 14.
2. Ellen White, *The Desire of Ages,* page 660.
3. V. T. Houteff, *Timely Greetings,* page 7.
4. Ellen White, *God's Amazing Grace,* page 42.
5. E. J. Waggoner, *Waggoner on Romans,* 5.101.
6. *The SDA Bible Commentary,* Ellen G. White Comments, vol. 1, p. 1085.

CHAPTER FOURTEEN

Can These Bones Live?

When I first began to study righteousness by faith, I felt similarly to the way I felt upon discovering Adventism. It was a sense of awe, as if I had discovered buried treasure or cracked a code that would open a vault full of blessings. I believed it was the answer to the stymied condition of Laodicea. Knowing that "a flood of light would have been shed upon the world . . . the closing work would have been completed, and Christ would have come," if the message had been embraced in 1888, I began to look forward to a time when a rediscovery of the message would bring about those very things. In fact, I still do.

But I have come to recognize that a mere intellectual grasp of the facts of the gospel is not enough to bring the needed changes. I have been disappointed with myself and with other people who have high conceptions of truth. As a whole, those who believe and teach the concepts I have shared in this book are just as faulty as anyone is. I have no boast to make in terms of understanding of the truth producing impressive results in character and life. Why not bigger and better changes in all of us?

The text that comes to mind in answer to this plea is found in John 4:23; " 'the true worshipers shall worship the Father in *spirit and truth' "* (emphasis mine). Jesus spoke these words to the woman of apostate Samaria, informing her of two things; " 'You worship that which you do not know. We worship that which we know, for salvation is from the Jews' " (v. 22). He was telling her that her religion did not have the correct facts and that the Jewish nation *did* have the correct facts, the "oracles of God," (Romans 3:2). He made no mention of the Jews having the correct *spirit,* and a basic perusal of their motives and methods reveals that they had anything but. Here was a woman whose receptive heart housed more of God's Spirit than a thousand "theologically correct" Pharisees, but the poor girl needed information, and badly. How could He access that information to her when those who had the information effectively dammed it up, especially from Samaritans?

Thus is the age-old dilemma. Both information (truth) and demonstration (spirit) are needed for true worship and witness of God. One without the other will lead to lopsided religion and eventually apostasy.

God longs to impart truth. He hears the prayer of the seeker and says, "if you cry out for discernment, and lift up your voice for understanding, if you seek her as silver, and search for her as for hidden treasures; then you will understand the fear of the Lord, and find the knowledge of God" (Proverbs 2:3-5, NKJV). He rejoices to convey vital information to the receptive heart. But in so doing, He takes a risk, for "knowledge puffs up" (1 Corinthians 8:1, NKJV). The acquirement of facts brings with it a price tag—the danger of the facts themselves becoming the means of inflated self-esteem, and therefore, a wall of separation between the ones who have the truth and those who need it.

Sad Stories

A friend of mine came to hear a gifted and knowledgeable speaker. In front of a crowd, the man shone like a burning light as truth-filled words about God's love literally poured out of him. My friend was so moved by the presentation that he felt an understandable urge to greet the messenger and affirm his ministry. When he did so, however, he felt as if an Arctic front had just rolled in. A cold, indifferent look and apathetic words told him in no uncertain terms that the man was not interested in talking to him. Though the preacher was filled with words about God's self-giving love, they lost their meaning somewhere between the pulpit and the people.

A wealthy woman attends a city church. She owns a gorgeous house, which she opens up for "important" company, but when common folks come to call, she feels invaded in a way they can sense. Soon the common folks realize that they are not welcome at this fine house, but often they hear this woman open up her mouth and speak about God's free gift of grace abounding to the world. Somehow, the teaching is lost on them because she keeps most of her "free grace" to herself.

A pastor wishes he understood righteousness by faith better, but there is a woman in his congregation who claims to have an edge on it, and she has done more to avert the curious pastor than draw him in. She condemns every outreach plan and ministry idea that is proposed and reads the pastor the riot act after every sermon, never finding so much as one point she can agree with. The pastor is almost to the point where he doesn't want to know *anything* about the 1888 message. This woman is intent upon preaching unique views of justification, but seems to minister condemnation wherever she goes.

Another group, who feel that they have special light in many areas, are afraid to attend potlucks because they might eat something "unkosher." Even when the church members try to make something these folks will eat, they won't touch it. These same people never open up and share during prayer time when others are relating their needs and concerns. As anxious as these people feel to preach the truth that Christ became "one of us," they have trouble incarnating themselves into even their own humanity and being one with their brothers and sisters.

These scenarios are sad! (Are they true? I won't say, but if the shoe fits, wear it!) Although some reports of "divisiveness" are based more on prejudice toward people with a distinctive view than they are based on any misbehavior on their part, some of the reports of "Gospel Pharisees" are true. For this I apologize in their behalf, knowing I too have failed to personify the truth as it is in Jesus. As we carry a message of cutting and controversial truth, our attitude should be, "I haven't failed if I am rejected because of the truth, but I *have* failed if the truth is rejected because of me."

But haven't most of us fallen into the same condemnation? Adventism as a whole has a history of being "heady," fact-oriented, left-brained. Some of the information we have been entrusted with is of the most sensitive and inflammatory character, such as the identity of the mark of the beast. How important that we impart our cutting message in the most Christlike fashion, lest we turn people from the very present truth they need to hear! I was so cheered to find that A. T. Jones, as "heady" a fellow as he was, saw this dilemma as well:

> One of the characteristics of the last days [is that] people will be *heady*; that is, they have their knowledge in their *heads*. But God wants *hearty* people in these days. Instead of people having the big *head*, he wants them to have a big *heart*. . . . There is entirely too much theory among Seventh-day Adventists, and not enough experience of the love of Christ in the heart; too much dogma, and not enough of the Spirit of God.[1]

The Two Parts of Truth: Structure and Spirit

Think of truth as a human body. When God made man, He fashioned an exquisite masterpiece of structure. Each cell had a framework, and cells comprised tissues. Tissues comprised organs, organs worked in systems. All the components were in place, but the body did not live until God breathed into it the spirit of life.

What happens when the spirit is taken away? At first the structure of the body holds, and there is a passage of time when the body looks alive but in fact is dead. Gradually, however, the body begins to decay and at last, structure itself erodes until all that is left is a multitude of bacteria and the dead matter they are feeding on amidst bare bones. Finally, gradually, even the bones decompose.

When God made truth, He likewise fashioned an exquisite masterpiece of structure, but truth housed in the mind is like Adam's inanimate body lying on Eden's soil. Not until the truth in the head meets the Spirit of Christ in the heart does that synergy make it "truth as it is in Jesus." *This* is the truth God wishes us to give to the world.

"Search heaven and earth, and there is no truth revealed more powerful than that which is made manifest in works of mercy to those who need our sympathy and aid. This is the truth as it is in Jesus."[2]

The truth is *revealed* in *actions* that involve *sympathy.* Not only is there tangible help, but there is a heartfelt connection to the ones being helped. A terse way of saying this might be: Preaching the truth involves more than the mouth and the mind. It involves the heart and the body.

If the Spirit does not enliven the structure of truth, the structure itself will eventually decay, with the bare-bones framework, the skeleton, being the last to break down. Just as no body can live without breath, no man, woman, or child can retain a theoretical knowledge of the truth indefinitely without allowing it to infuse itself into the motivational center of their being. The theory will degrade over time until its original form is undefinable, except a frightening, useless theological skeleton. When all that is left of the message we are to bear is dry bones, the truth loses its power to draw (unless you are a fellow skeleton).

Imagine a stage upon which shines a beaming spotlight. The announcer's voice proclaims that the winner of the Miss. Universe beauty pageant is behind the curtain. The timpani rolls while the violins build up to a crescendo. The audience is breathless. With a symbol crash the curtain is yanked open to reveal . . . the skeleton of Miss. Universe. What does the audience do? It shudders in fear, at least. Several women scream, and children run out of the auditorium. Disgruntled people start lining up for a ticket refund.

Such is the effect of a skeletal structure upon the mind—it frightens and repels. The theory of truth is like bones in that they are inseparable from truth manifest in the flesh. A dogmatic observance of the Sabbath, an argumentative approach to doctrines, health reform carried out with self-defeating stressfulness, these are like so many dry bones rattling in the desert sun.

> In all human experience a theoretical knowledge of truth has been proved to be insufficient for the saving of the soul. It does not bring forth the fruits of righteousness.[3]

Amazingly, the vessels of dry theory often become aggressive toward those who live the truth:

> A jealous regard for what is termed theological truth often

accompanies a hatred for genuine truth as made manifest in the life.[4]

For the proponents of justification by faith to have a Pharisaic spirit is the greatest travesty that could possibly be. This is a message that was designed to "lay the glory of man in the dust."[5] If knowledge of the message of 1888 is used as a reason to be "puffed up," then it is bringing about the very opposite result God designed it should bring. Christ's call to Laodicea is based on the fact that she thinks she has "become wealthy" and is really unaware that she is " ' "wretched and miserable and poor and blind and naked" ' " (Revelation 3:17). Part of our "wealth" is the cache of spiritual light that God has bequeathed to us. Wouldn't the Laodecian message, then, have a double application to anyone among us that believes they have a special understanding of truth?

How can we hear and believe something as pure and holy as the righteousness by faith message and become prideful and exclusive about it? The message reveals that we are nothing! To attempt to use it as a means of making something of ourselves is approximately as productive as eating dust. Still, pride can burn very hot in the human heart with oh, so little to fan the flame.

Any unique insight we possess, any special knowledge imparted to us of heaven makes us debtors to those around us with lesser light and understanding. We *owe* them a witness of what God has given us. Should we lord it over those we are indebted to? This was the pattern the Pharisees fell into—they allowed truth to become a means of elevating themselves above the Gentiles, rather than a means of humbling them with a sense of responsibility. If we allow our doctrines and beliefs to cater to our sense of superiority we are giving the most conclusive proof that we have lost the spirit of truth. It will only be a matter of time before we are skeletons.

But there is hope. Even dry bones can once again be clothed with flesh and infused with the breath of life (see Ezekiel 37:1-14). "Can these bones live?" The answer is "they can." We know from the story of Nicodemus that even Pharisees can repent.

Some of us might be faulted on the opposite score. We shun the investigation of deep and potentially controversial truths, all the while proclaiming that all that matters is that "the heart is in the right place."

If the truth was known, many of us who speak these words are motivated more by a lazy mind than a loving heart. While truth without spirit degrades until finally truth itself is dead, spirit without truth is equally degrading. Head without heart will eventually lead to the corruption of head knowledge, but heart without head will eventually lead to decadence of spirit. Truth and spirit, head and heart, are dependent upon one another for life.

It is possible to *temporarily* have wrong information but the right motives and spirit? Mary Magdalene is a good example of this—she took the ointment she originally bought for Jesus' burial and poured it over Him at Simon's party. She was led astray by the disciples' false teaching that "he was about to be crowned king," but her motives were that "she was eager to be first in honoring her Lord."[6] Mary, however, was at the feet of Jesus every spare moment of her life, willing to learn all she could. She did not refuse greater light when it came, in fact she pursued it. If she had rested content with what she knew, the fire inside her would eventually have died out.

Emotions play a part in true worship, but they are awakened by God-given thoughts; in other words, the heart is reached through the head. Many influences in the world work on the opposite principle, accessing the thoughts through the emotions, and particularly the primal emotions such as fear, survival, and mating—which is why media is saturated with violence, consumerism, and sex. The media works through dramatic, musical, and visual stimuli to access the emotions, because it is emotion that drives attention. Once the emotions are accessed and defenses are down, the television and other media are powerful to mold values and thinking. Unfortunately, the bulk of media productions infuse the world's value system rather than heaven's, for "all that is in the world—the lust of the flesh, the lust of the eyes, and the pride of life—is not of the Father but is of the world" (1 John 2:16, NKJV).

Spirit without truth leads to emotionalism, which is increasingly the bane of the religious world. Because they are designed to attract media-saturated masses, religious services often attempt to match the emotional charge of a major motion picture or a playoff game. The same breaking down of defenses can occur in a church setting as occurs in media viewing, and with the subsequent molding of thoughts and morals. This phenomenon is no new thing, having been an important feature of idol worship in biblical times, when music and other art forms were used to bypass reason and lead the populous into sin. (See Exodus 32 and Daniel 3.) True worshipers of God would do well, as always, to avoid emotional stimulus without a basis of conviction, regardless of how religious it may appear to be. We must not allow anyone to manipulate our emotions then do our thinking for us.

Human beings seem prone to two extremes, intellectualization of truth and reducing religion to an emotional high. Both fail to secure that vital connection between head and heart, which results in practical godliness. But if we as a Church are guilty of one more than the other, it is the intellectualization of our message—at least I can speak for myself in saying that. My prayer is that our dry bones of doctrine will very soon be clothed with warm, willing human flesh.

Mahatma Ghandi said to a crowd of church leaders, "When you Christians live as your Master did, all of India will bow down to you."[7] In response to a Christian's effort to convert him, he replied, "From the point of view of sacrifice, it seemed to me that the Hindus greatly surpassed the Christians."[8] In the absence of living, flesh-and-blood proof, the truths of Christianity seem to an onlooking world like a bunch of outlandish claims created to advance the cause of a religious institution. Maybe he's right. Maybe we don't get it.

And maybe the only answer for Ghandi and the millions like him will come when these bones live.

> The theory of truth "puffs up."
> The spirit of truth "lays the glory of man in the dust."

> The theory of truth will gratify insiders and frighten outsiders.
> The spirit of truth will humble insiders and draw outsiders.

> The theory of truth hates the spirit of truth.
> The spirit of truth loves the truth completely.

> The theory of truth uses truth to elevate itself above fellow sinners.

The spirit of truth feels a humble responsibility toward fellow sinners.

The theory of truth makes us "rich and increased with goods."

The spirit of truth makes us debtors to those who don't know the truth.

The theory of truth rests satisfied with what it has until it has nothing.

The spirit of truth searches for more until it has Everything.

1. A. T. Jones, *General Conference Bulletin,* 1995, page 173.
2. Ellen White, *Thoughts From the Mount of Blessing,* page 137.
3. Ellen White, *The Desire of Ages,* page 309.
4. Ibid.
5. Ellen White, *Testimonies to Ministers,* page 456.
6. Ellen White, *Desire of Ages,* page 559.
7. A personal interview with an eyewitness.
8. The Official Mahatma Ghandi Web site, <http://www.mahatma.org.in/antho.htm>. "Religious Ferment."

CHAPTER FIFTEEN

Finally, a Flood of Light

Mary's hands stroke the feet of the Master as thick, sweet rivers run down her wrists and soak into the dirt floor. No one notices her until the room is filled with a fragrance which drifts into their consciousness and registers its identity in two phases; "spikenard" first, then "hundreds of denarii, a life savings." In spite of their austere living conditions, the disciples of the One who made Himself poor that they might be made rich still know the smell of money.

Their eyes fall upon the whimpering form on the floor before the Master. They see shards of alabaster, then notice glistening oil all over Him; His beard, face, shoulders, feet. They piece together the facts of this pathetic scene and moan inside themselves with embarrassment.

Judas is the first to speak. His scorn is laden with guilt. "She has deprived the poor," he says, "she has hurt the already hurting."

Being intimately acquainted with hurt, Mary trembles at the implication. *Could it be?* She begins to shrink away when suddenly she hears the Voice.

"Leave her alone," He says. "She has done all she could." Mary's tears drop from her hanging head and dot the floor, almost audibly now that the room is stone silent.

A woman? A woman with a past? He has stooped to defend her?

The questions hang unanswered except by the obvious. At her knees lay the broken alabaster box, evidence of a love-crime that cost her a year's wages. She is caught in the act of loving God without restraint.

She scans through the motives that led to her act. He forgave her for years of selling her body. He delivered her from seven devils, hunting her down seven times until she was finally willing to give up everything, even her precious bitterness, because He loved her soul. Love was all she had ever wanted from anyone, and here was One who gave it, a man no less. The real item, not some indulgent counterfeit cloaked in tenderness.

She heard Him speak of dying for the sins of the world, and in her sorrow, she groped for some way to honor Him. According to the Law of Moses, the wages of a prostitute were not to be used as an offering. But she could use those wages to buy a gift, and thus, the alabaster box full of precious ointment. It cost her everything she had.

Then at Simon's feast she heard them say that He was soon to be king. *Oh, yes,* she thought with joy, *then I can honor Him as such.* Out came the box, but when it broke, her heart broke with it as if they were one and the same. A total loss of composure followed: a wet face contorted with emotion, a body shaken by sobbing, an irrepressible display of affection. The fragrance filled the room the way He had filled her soul, but with this difference: Her offering provoked shame in them while His offering provoked praise in her. The scent of love has a way of dividing the world into two classes.

Now the Voice was defending her in the presence of those that would turn her out onto the street if they could. He tells them that her act is to be proclaimed wherever His gospel is preached. Again, stunned, stone silence.

The implication is too much for Judas. He is smarting with the rebuke, long-held antipathy smouldering in his eyes. He broods . . . *can He commend this waste of a human being and in the process censure me?*

The spirit is contagious until Simon's eyes catch the same glare. *Doesn't He know what a vile thing she is? Why does He let her touch Him?*

Mary smarts under the injustice. The very one who ruptured her innocence thinks himself superior to his victim. It isn't the first time the perpetrator has lorded it over the prey, and it won't be the last. But she has tasted this irony too long. *Let it go, let it go.* She is pure again; she knows it. *Feel pity for him who doesn't.*

Now the Voice speaks a parable. Two debtors, one owing ten times more. Both forgiven. "Who," He asks, "should love the most?"

"The one whom he forgave the most," Simon mutters, knowing in that instant that he is apprehended. The sweat glands in this guilty one's face explode, paling him to a gray-white. It is as if a supernatural Glance has pierced his skin and inspected the secret rooms of his soul—the dark, defensive rooms where there is no light, no air. As the Eyes probe, he feels a flicker of despair and corresponding rage. He is ready to retreat into his secret room again, to slam the door to the light, when he sees something in the Eyes that arrest him.

They have more than all power. They have all love.

A wonder comes to pass. Reality comes rushing into Simon's consciousness. He understands that Jesus knows his great sin, yet does not expose nor shame him. Time warps for a moment as love and sin meet face to face; but there is no contest because there is no resistance. Sin disintegrates and love triumphs. For the first time since he ruined his life and hers, Simon feels safe to break into a million fragments. He who could have snapped in brittleness shatters in remorse.

He casts a glance at Mary, the living monument of his shame. Suddenly, she is the powerful one and he the suppliant. *Would she forgive him too?* The humble slant of her shoulders, the grateful sorrow on her face, speak *yes, yes, she will.*

Impossible healing has begun.

The spectacle unfolds. The broken box has marked its trail and the ensuing river of grace will flow over all that it touches. For ages to come it will be told, the story of this broken woman and her broken box. Here are the first-fruits of the power of her witness, the ability of God working through a human heart to flip the misery of sin on it's axis and make that very sin an opportunity to prove grace. Mary was Simon's victim. Simon is Mary's convert. Love was crucified by humanity. Humanity is saved by Love. Who can resist the call to partake of the great exchange?

Mary the Mirror

For a moment in time, Mary Magdalene was a mirror of Christ. Her worship was so pure, so selfless, that He could point to her act and know that He would shine through it. He did not say that her deed should be proclaimed "wherever this gospel is preached" because it would supplement or garnish the gospel story, but because it would underscore it. In telling her story side by side with His, it is as if He wanted to say, "Mary's act of sacrifice and mine are of the same character. She has echoed without words every word I have ever spoken. Her actions have reflected mine. My story shows what I did *for* people, Mary's story shows what I can do *in* people. Look at her and you will see Me."

Mary was also a prototype of the bride of Christ. Someday, (oh please, someday soon), a people will reflect Him so gloriously that He will be able to showcase them before the world knowing that the world will see only Him. It will not be fiberoptics or satellites or computer technology advances that finally spread the message of the gospel to every living creature, it will be love personified. God will know when His people are ready, and He will arrange the needed connections that they might access the living truth to the entire globe.

Does it seem presumptuous to say that sinners can ever reflect a holy God so fully? The story of Mary Magdalene gives evidence that it is not, for Jesus Himself would then be presumptuous. He was the One who commanded that attention be given to her deed, not to glorify man, for "all flesh is grass" but to glorify God. Why else would He give her such prime time exposure? Consider these predictions:

> " 'Wherever this gospel is preached *in the whole world,* what this woman has done will also be told as a memorial to her' " (Matthew 26:13, NKJV, emphasis mine).

> " 'This gospel of the kingdom will be preached *in all the world* as a witness to all the nations, and then the end will come' " (Matthew 24:14, NKJV, emphasis mine).

> " 'Go *into all the world* and preach the gospel to every creature' " (Mark 16:15, NKJV, emphasis mine).

Someday every living inhabitant of the earth—the whole world—will have heard the gospel. They will also have heard about Mary. Yes, someday the entire globe will know about two individuals: Jesus Christ and Mary Magdalene.

Refine that a little further. The focal point of the gospel, even the gospel itself, is the Cross. This means that someday every man, woman, and child will know about two acts of self-giving love: Christ's and Mary's.

What was it about Mary's gift of precious ointment that reflected Heaven's Gift of the spotless Son? The parallels between the cross of Christ and the gift of Mary are clear.

1. They both created a far-reaching influence:

Christ's cross was "an offering and a sacrifice to God for a sweet-smelling aroma" (Ephesians 5:2, NKJV).

Mary's gift was "a pound of very costly oil of spikenard. . . . And the house was filled with the fragrance of the oil" (John 12:3, NKJV).

2. They were both extremely valuable:

Christ's cross was where we were "redeemed . . . with the precious blood of Christ" (1 Peter 1:18,19, NKJV).

Mary's ointment was, "very costly," and " 'might have been sold for more than three hundred denarii,' " (Mark 14:3, 5, NKJV). One denarii was about a day's wages (see Matthew 20:2), making Mary's purchase worth about a year's wages.

3. They were both extravagant:

Christ's cross was a seeming waste, but "it could not be restricted so as not to exceed the number who would accept the great gift."[1]

Mary's gift likewise seemed like a squandering of resources and provoked the words, " 'Why this waste?' " (Matthew 26:8).

4. They both prompted scorn:

Christ's cross hung in the midst of mocking rulers, Romans soldiers, and people. Jesus was, "a reproach of men, and despised of the people." He said, "All those who see Me ridicule Me" (Psalm 22:6, 7, NKJV).

Mary's gift brought the same scorn, for "when His disciples saw it, they were indignant" (Matthew 26:8, NKJV).

5. They were both vessels forever broken:

Christ's cross gave Him wounds that will always remain, significant of His eternal identification with humanity. (See John 20:27; Zechariah 13:6.)

Mary's gift was contained in an alabaster box that, once broken, could never be resealed.[2]

6. They both led some that were present to repentance:

Christ's cross induced Simon of Cyrene to "take the cross from choice,"[3] the thief on the cross to say, " 'Lord, remember me when You come into Your kingdom' " (Luke 23:42, NKJV), the Roman soldier to say, " 'Truly this was the Son of God!' " (Matthew 27:54, NKJV).

Mary's gift led to the conversion of Simon, who "became a lowly, self-sacrificing disciple."[4]

7. They both led some to seal their fate:

Christ's cross led to the Jewish nation's complete rejection of God when they cried, " 'We have no king but Caesar' " (John 19:15).

Mary's gift led to Judas's complete rejection of Christ, for "from the supper he went directly to the palace of the high priest, where he . . . offered to betray Christ into their hands."[5]

8. They both led many afterward to salvation:

Christ's cross will draw "a great multitude, which no one could count " who will "[stand] before the throne and before the Lamb" (Revelation 7:9).

Mary's gift would "shed its fragrance" wherever the gospel was preached, and "until time should be no more, that broken alabaster box would tell the story of the abundant love of God for a fallen race."[6]

9. They both manifested true, love-motivated faith:

Christ's cross was the pinnacle of His expression of the love of God, which He brought to us through utter darkness when "By faith, Christ was the victor."[7] "The faith of Jesus" is a faith that works "through love" (Revelation 14:12; Galatians 5:6, NKJV).

Mary's gift was a response of gratitude to the love of Jesus for her soul. Jesus said, " 'Your faith has saved you; go in peace' " (Luke 7:50).

There is more. The Bible predicts a witness at the end of earth's shortening days that will also reflect the Great Offering of God in His Son. A whole army of Mary Magdalenes will arise out of the swamp of human sin, bearing the lily-white righteousness of Christ. God will work through us once again to speak to the world of His mercy.

Our offerings can never equal the pattern of Calvary, but they can follow it. Jesus was unafraid to draw attention to what Mary did, and He is still in search of those He can shine through without obstruction. Someday, the collective witness of His church will produce a picture of His grace so exquisite that the entire earth will be illuminated with knowledge of the love of God. Do you want to be a part of it for His sake?

"The church is the depositary of the wealth of the riches of the grace of Christ, and through the church eventually will be made manifest the final and full display of the love of God to the world that is to be lightened with its glory" (TTM 50)

Far-reaching, precious, extravagant, scorn-surrounded, broken forever, prompting repentance, sealing fate, leading to salvation, powered by love-motivated faith. This is the Cross, this was the offering of Mary, this will be the final witness of God's people.

> Their message will be far-reaching, extending to the whole world.
>
> Their witness will be powered by the precious gold of *agape* love.
>
> It will be extravagant, reaching every soul, but refused by the majority.
>
> They will worship God in the midst of scorn that mounts to persecution.
>
> They will be broken in spirit, completely delivered from self-sufficiency.
>
> They will lead those around them toward repentance because they model it.
>
> Their message will prompt some to seal their fate in rejecting God.
>
> Their ministry to the world will lead multitudes to worship the true God.
>
> They will be characterized by a faith that is motivated by love.

This is the hope to which we are tightly tethered. God will one day fill humankind with His fullness and use us in the consummation of the ages, the final showdown of the great controversy.

In the beginning of the war, Satan declared that justice destroyed mercy, that sin could not be forgiven. When the Cross disproved this claim, Satan asserted that mercy destroyed justice, that the death of Christ had changed God's law. This charge still lingers in the air, and it can only be refuted by God working through His followers. They will prove the immutability of the law by obeying it, not only in total, but in spirit. Right down to the substrata of their beings, the law of love will be written, engraved on every soul-fiber, impressed on every heart-cell. Through their living testimony God will declare the perfect harmony between mercy and justice, a harmony Satan has passionately sought to obscure.

Once the proclamation of the third angel's message reaches every ear, the line will be drawn between the true and false gospel; between God's law and man's; between selfless love and self-love; between liberty and coercion. No changes of mind will take place after Jesus shouts, "It is done!" The great experiment of sin will have proven it to be wholly detestable, and God to be wholly worthy of worship and adoration. The faith of God that sinners and sin would be forever separated will bear fruit in that reality. Finally, a people will mirror His cross, which will lighten the earth with His glory.

1. Ellen White, *The Desire of Ages,* page 566.
2. Ibid., page 559.
3. Ibid., page 742.
4. Ibid., page 568.
5. Ibid., page 564.
6. Ibid., page 563.
7. Ibid., page 756.

If you enjoyed this book, you'll enjoy this one by the same author:

Testimony of a Seeker
Jennifer Jill Schwirzer. The autobiography of a young woman's journey to grace.
0-8163-1769-0. US$12.99, Cdn$19.49.

Other products by Jennifer Jill Schwirzer:

Chance of Rain
Jennifer Jill. Songs of Christ's passion to save and fill us. Songs include "Gethsemane Angel," "Anathema; The God-Forsaken God," "Were You There?" "In Christ Medley," "Chance of Rain," and others. CD:4-3330-0218-4; C: 4-3330-0218-5. US$15.98, Cdn$23.99.

Gospel Moments
Jennifer Jill. Stories, songs and scriptures that teach children about salvation. Five cassettes, US$6.98, Cdn$10.49 each, or US$29.98, Cdn$44.99 for entire 5 volume set.
Vol. 1: God's Love and Christ's Humanity. C:4-3330-0074-6.
Vol. 2: The Sanctuary and Joy in Trials. C:4-3330-0074-8.
Vol. 3: The Power of Faith and Beholding Christ. C:4-3330-0074-9.
Vol. 4: Mary Magdalene and the Motive of Love. C:4-3330-0075-0.
Vol. 5: Christ's Coming, Heaven and the New Covenant: C:4-3330-0075-1.
    5 Vol. Set: C:4-3330-0075-2.

Order from your ABC by calling **1-800-765-6955**, or get online and shop our virtual store at **<www.adventistbookcenter.com>**.

•Read a chapter from your favorite book
•Order online
•Sign up for email notices on new products

Prices subject to change without notice.